KOREA,

Her Story

KORVEA,

Her Story

COMPILED BY
ADRIENNE HARRELL

Library of Congress Control Number:		2013904539
ISBN:	Hardcover	978-1-4836-0709-2
	Softcover	978-1-4836-0708-5
	Ebook	978-1-4836-0710-8

This book was printed in the United States of America.

Rev. date: 01/27/2014

To order additional copies of this book, contact:
Xlibris LLC
1-888-795-4274
www.Xlibris.com
Orders@Xlibris.com
553522

FOREWORD

The Korean War has been called the Forgotten War. Americans were tired of war, anxious to return to peacetime. This conflict came too close on the heels of World War II. The United States was never strongly involved in Korea. What was going on halfway around the world was ignored by most of the country. But a small segment of the population felt the effect of this call to arms. For some, the war was all too real.

This is a chronicle of a time in military wives' past. Some of the wives' responses may seem strange to young readers who grew up at a later time. Those of us who were young in Depression and war times had very different experiences than theirs. There was still a housing shortage. A lot of rent properties were ramshackle and inadequate, but hard to find, at that.

Our generation of young women was teenagers during a shortage of gasoline, cars, and tires. We did not have the opportunity to do much driving.

Patriotism, self-sacrifice, and dedication were philosophies we understood. We had watched our older sisters wait for their men to return. We had seen the havoc despotism could wreak on the world.

We married young. Most of us were not really prepared to keep house, cook, or parent, but we married for keeps—even though we probably did not fully understand what that might involve. We did understand that we were expected to stay in the background and be reticent. Bear up!

Lifestyles were very different. Few wives worked. Most couples were lucky to own a car. Not many owned washing machines. Washing diapers was a daily chore, along with hanging them on the line, then folding them. Baby formula was mixed and then sterilized, along with water. The work didn't stop us from having babies. The boom was on!

Our romantic dream was of an idyllic family life. That would have to wait. Our turn had come to sacrifice.

Many thanks to the wives who have generously shared their memories, and many thanks to those who have encouraged me and assisted me—especially to Jim Harrell, my son. He felt these memoirs are part of his legacy, as they are of all our families.

Adrienne Harrell

CONTRIBUTORS

Virginia "Gin" Watterson
Eloise Knox Adams
Adrienne Harrell
Constance "Connie" Shepherd
Billie Jo Harvey Nolan
Lois Mitchell
Mary Jane Sullivan, PhD
Caroline Schreier
Henrietta "Boots" Hansen
Margery Ritchart
Winona Smelt
Eleanor Carmichael
Pat Lennon
Louise Schryver
Winifred "Wyn" Van Cleve Kelley
Joyce Stuart
Jeanne Stemple
Meta J. Reed
Betty Moore
Mary Gratzer Bush
Barbara "Bobbie" Doezema
Gladys "Babs" Rudzis
Anna "Peggy" Salvo
Doris "Dorie" Carper
Laura L. Reeves
Barbara Reid Sorenson
Dorothy "Dot" Fredericks
Mary White Lucy
Betty J. Lees
Elizabeth "Betty" Bey
Estelle Deptula ("Talents")

2 April 1998

Dear Adrienne,

Received your letter concerning the time the Korean War began and our husbands went over to become part of the United Nations Forces to restore peace. It was so very long ago yet some memories are still remarkably clear in my mind.

Don, the children, Jon 5 years & Judy 1 1/2 years, and myself had returned from Guam early in 1950 with the 1st Brigade, 5th Marines to Camp Pendleton. A violent typhoon the end of November the previous year had devastated Camp Witek on Guam, wrecking most of the buildings and many of the quarters.

Rather than rebuild the base, the powers-that-be decided to close it down and send everyone back to the continental U.S. In January, the children and I embarked on the Randall, one of the two ships taking dependents home. Don followed a month later with the men of the Brigade.

Once Don rejoined us in California, we were assigned quarters in Homaja, a large housing area of Quonset huts just inside the main gate at Camp Pendleton. The quarters consisted of half a Quonset, furnished, 2 bedrooms, living/dining room, small kitchen and a bath. Life settled down to be fairly normal. Don was still with the 1st Brigade. We had many friends who had been on Guam with us, and we made new friends in Homaja. Dot Fredericks, a neighbor, became a special friend, along with Dorie Carper and Kay Mars.

At the outbreak of the Korean War, 25 June 1950, we knew within days that the 1st Brigade would be going. Don spent his last few evenings at home patiently trying to teach me to drive our 1949 DeSoto convertible. Although he had tried to instruct me many times in the years before, I had no great desire or incentive to learn until this crises arose. Now I needed to get my license. On my 26th birthday, 15 July 1950, Don boarded a ship in San Diego with the rest of the 1st Brigade to sail for Korea. Life took on a waiting game, waiting for news, waiting for mail, waiting for our men to return.

A few weeks later, those of us living in Homaja where told to vacate our Quonsets by 1 September. The reserve Marines were pouring into Camp Pendleton from all over the country, and the need was critical to house those who brought their families. So we hunted for places to rent in nearby Oceanside. I found a small 2 bedroom duplex in South Oceanside on Freeman Street. Having always lived in furnished government quarters, we had only acquired a few items of baby furniture, a washing machine and refrigerator. Now I began to turn packing boxes into tables and buying basic furniture for the duplex, a few pieces at a time. The Marine Corps moved me over Labor Day weekend. My immediate neighbors were Kay and Joyce Ray. Kay had been instrumental in helping me find the duplex next to hers.

Friends from Guam, Martha Ann, Jean and Maxine, lived in Oceanside or Carlsbad. Dot Fredericks, with her young baby Wendy, found a beach house in Oceanside not far away from my place. We saw each other often.

Our financial situation was the same as all the other First Lieutenant's and Captain's wives—slim but adequate. Being frugal and not wasting money had come naturally to most of the Marine wives since we had grown up during the depression years. Fresh fruits and vegetables were plentiful and cheap in Southern California. We shopped mainly at the commissary on the base for staples and meats. I remember eating a lot of tuna noodle casseroles!

Most of my time was spent with the children and caring for them but we frequently got together with friends and their children for hot dog roasts on the beach, swimming at the base pool or other outings. There were pot luck dinners, bridge games and an occasional drive-in movie, with the children bundled up in pajamas and blankets in the back seat. And always there were letters to write, to husbands and to family back home. Mail was important. I wrote Don every day, he tried to do the same. His letters always seemed to come in bunches. They were our lifeline to each other. No e-mail or internet in those days!

As wives of young Marine officers, we never once thought of complaining to any Marine Corps authority or asking for assistance. I did not feel alone—all my friends were in the same situation. We were strong support for each other. None of us had jobs outside the home—our job was to care for the children and keep the home running smoothly. There was no whining or 'poor me' attitude. Those feelings better describe a later generation and a later war. We were proud of our husbands and knew they were doing a job that needed to be done. That's not to say we were Polly Annas, we certainly had our low moments and dark days, but we somehow got through them without bitterness towards the world. The other wives were there to help lift the blues, give a helping hand or a shoulder to cry on; we were there for each other. And we prayed a lot.

The first dark time, for me, came a few weeks after Don left, when our son Jon fell one morning cutting a deep gash in his thigh on a rusty nail. I still hadn't gotten my driver's license but knew I had to get medical help so I put the kids in the car and drove the 7 or 8 miles to the base hospital. It was Saturday morning, the hospital and staff were preparing for a big inspection team and not happy to see an emergency. After finally getting someone's attention, Jon was hurried in to be treated and stitched up. As the doctor was putting in the stitches, he asked me about a large soft lump which had developed on the inside of Jon's knee. The doctor immediately sent Jon to be x-rayed, suspecting the lump was a cancerous tumor. For the next few weeks a team of doctors were in doubt as to the kind of tumor and whether the leg could be saved. Jon was operated on mid-September by the head of the orthopedic department to remove the lump after the infected gash had healed. It proved to be only a fatty cyst caused by a bruise but rarely seen in young children.

Friends had taken care of Judy during the many trips to the hospital with Jon. Jean, bless her heart, had taken it upon herself to finish my driving lessons and

I passed the driver's test to be a legal driver. Jon had recovered and went back to school as a first grader.

That September during the invasion of Inchon, Don was wounded by a piece of shrapnel that pierced his helmet and helmet liner, entering his temple. He was treated by a medic and returned to the battle. The first news I had of this injury was in a letter from Don who made light of the incident. It was one year later that I received notification from Headquarters Marine Corps that my husband had been wounded. I still have the penny sized piece of jagged shrapnel in my jewelry box.

The darkest time for almost all the wives of the 1st Brigade Marines was early in December when the men were coming out of North Korea from the Chosen Reservoir after the Chinese armies invaded. It was days before I learned that Don had survived the Chinese attack and made it safely to Hungnam harbor, where they boarded ships for Pusan in Southern Korea. The network of wives helped keep our spirits up and support each other. Our fervent prayers were answered that all the close friends had come through virtually unscathed. It was a joyful Christmas knowing our husbands were safe even if we were apart.

In January my parents drove out from Michigan to spend a few weeks with the children and myself. Then the end of February, Jon came down with the mumps, and Judy a few weeks later.

Dot and I got word in early March that our husbands were coming home. We decided to go to San Francisco to meet the ship due on the 22nd of

March. Don's mother came out by train from Chicago to take care of the children, who were recovering from mumps. After making reservations at the Marine Memorial Club in Frisco, Dot and I set out up the coast. She drove the entire way, covering over 500 miles in one day. We arrived giddy with happiness but weary from the long trip. I don't think either of us slept much that night. Early the next morning we were on the pier to welcome the Randall as it docked in Oakland with our husbands. Bud and Don were among the first off the ship for a very joyful reunion. That had to be one of the happiest days in our lives to be back together once again. It had been a long 8 months!!

Dot Fredericks and I became very close friends during those months our husbands were in Korea—it is a friendship I treasure and one that is just as strong to this day.

Best wishes,
Gin Watterson

ELOISE KNOX ADAMS

A dear friend of mine of many years has asked me to remember the long-ago days of 1950 and 1951—the time my husband, Nate Adams, was in Korea. It seems like yesterday, and the memories are crystal clear.

We had been looking forward to the summer of 1950. At last we could settle down like a regular married couple, enjoying each other and our baby, Hawes. Nate was to be stationed at Camp Lejeune, and we thought we'd be there for about three years. Little did we know that we'd be there for six weeks.

Nate returned from the Med cruise in June. We found a brand-new cottage on the inland waterway in Swansboro, North Carolina, about half an hour from Lejeune. It was right next door to a fish house.

Things suddenly changed, and we became familiar with a country named Korea. Our husbands were soon on their way. In fact, we said good-bye, and Nate left. He would be back home by Christmas, it was said. But big surprise! The trains didn't arrive to take the men to California, so they all came home for one more night. That was great for us as our son, Hawes, chose that night to walk, and his daddy was able to see him take his first step.

Nate was gone, and there I was with a young child and an old car I could not drive—the Green Hornet. My brother, Bob, came down to drive me back to Virginia, where I'd divide the time between Nate's parents and mine. One thing I remember vividly was that my brother insisted I buy a jack before he would start out. I objected, but to no avail. So I spent a large part of my limited cash on the jack, to my dismay.

Our neighbor was from California, and she was determined to get there before the troop train. She packed her car and left. I took care of the movers both at her house and ours. One couldn't help but feel lonely and concerned. But I felt Nate was a professional Marine and knew how to take care of himself and his men. He was doing the job he was trained and paid to do. Perhaps if my husband had been a reserve who was recalled and our life disrupted, I would have felt differently.

I took advantage of the time Nate was overseas. I learned to drive. Then I finished my last semester of college the end of May 1951. (I made a scrapbook from the newspaper articles.)

In August, Nate returned, and we were to go to Quantico. Housing was tight. We found a farmhouse outside of Fredericksburg to rent, but happily, I never had to get used to a woodstove as his orders were changed, and we went to Washington, DC.

ADRIENNE HARRELL

(MRS. JAMES E.)

Korea! This was our turn—our generation's war. Most of us had been too young for World War II. We experienced it through the news, radio, and those around us. Now the call had come for help from South Korea. We had watched Eastern Europe and China fall to the Communists. Once again our country was going to the aid of its allies.

The First Marine Brigade was heading out into the Pacific yet again. Their first job would be to drive the North Koreans back across the Pusan perimeter. The first job for their wives was, as always, to keep the home front going. That may not seem such a difficult task, but most of us were young and inexperienced at both marriage and the military.

I was no exception. Jim and I had gotten married when I was nineteen and he was twenty-two. Now, we were almost at our second anniversary when he got the news that he was going to Korea. It was the summer of 1950. As the wife of a career military man, I was not surprised. This was what could happen though, as wives, we all fervently hoped it never would.

The weeks before the men left were a blur. I do remember we went to a nightclub in San Diego and heard Nellie Lutcher sing. We danced. I floated in his arms.

Standing on my own two feet was something I had never done before. Back then, at the University of Texas, a female student was carefully tended with strict dorm and university rules. Other than the decision to get married, there had been few things I had done on my own. Now I had a long, blank space to fill while I waited for Jim to come home.

We had been living in Sterling Housing Apartments, which I had to vacate shortly after he left. I dealt with packers for the first time. We had acquired three rooms of newly married stuff. I remember a floor lamp and hooked rug—all of which would go in storage.

Since I could hardly drive more than to the grocery store and back, we sold our ancient Pontiac. It was nine years old when we bought it. I had no need for a car in a small town of two thousand five hundred. I could walk wherever I needed to go.

I was going back to Junction, Texas, and my parents on the Greyhound bus. It was a three-day trip. There was no baby, not even one expected. I went back to work in the hardware store my father and his brothers owned, along with a Ford agency. Extra money came in handy for me. My allotment out of my husband's paycheck of $350 didn't go far.

Eighteen—at the University of Texas—
a sophomore and engaged. Ain't life grand!

Meta Reed and Adrienne and Jim

The letters came regularly. We both wrote each other once a day. Then they stopped. No mail! The news worsened. No, it couldn't be! North of the 38th parallel, in a tiny corner of Korea, the UN troops were surrounded and cut off by the Communist Chinese! We heard that the situation was so critical the wounded were being left behind in a retreat back to the North Korean coast. Each day, I walked down to the hardware store and worked. I'd cross the street to the post office—no mail! Six weeks of this, and the tension was building. Thanksgiving came and went. Finally, a packet of letters reached me. He was okay! The dam burst! I sobbed. My aunt asked, "What's the matter with you?" I had to go home, overcome with pent-up emotion.

At that time, military wives' emotions and thoughts were best hidden. We knew to keep our feelings to ourselves. Careers could depend on it. Besides, what good did it do to complain? We had set ourselves up for separation and stress by marrying into the military. We could safely vent only to our own families or our peers.

Now I was happy and ready for Christmas. If only he were home, and if only my mother would leave me alone. She would start with

"I didn't want you to get married" and escalate to "I wish you'd get a divorce." Each day, I listened to this until I thought I was going to have a nervous breakdown.

Finally, I enrolled in the University of Texas to finish some of my required classes and to get away from my mother. I kept myself on a strict budget and was able to eat on $1 a day. Needless to say, I lost weight.

Wonderful news! The troops were coming back in March. Good-bye to UT! I caught the bus to San Francisco and met him at the dock. I think I got pregnant when the gangplank went down. Anyway, that's another story.

Back home, we drove our new convertible to Monterrey, Mexico. We stayed one night in a motel. At 6:00 a.m., a bugle sounded at a nearby army camp and woke us. Jim was up, looking for his rifle. The sound brought back unpleasant memories of Chinese bugles signaling a charge. He realized he was safe at home, and we could laugh in relief.

CONNIE SHEPHERD stayed at Camp Lejeune, North Carolina, in a mobile home with her kindergartener, Carole, when her husband was deployed to Korea. George and Connie had been married six years at that time.

"I was very young—only 18 in July when we married in 1944. I had finished high school in Jacksonville, FL where my Dad was stationed in the Navy. I worked as a civil service clerk typist at NAS Jacksonville, NAS Seattle and the Naval Training Station, San Diego. My mother and I followed my Dad."

A number of service wives stayed at Camp Lejeune when their husbands were sent to Korea. There were medical, PX, commissary, and recreational facilities available to families. Connie felt the environment was supportive during their thirteen-month separation.

"One thing—a small thing--really—they took away our base tags for the car. [In order to get on the military base, a car had to have an identifying tag or sticker.] We received a tiny windowshield sticker. It kept curling up and peeling off. A small irritant."

George was wounded at Yong Dong Po and evacuated to a hospital in Japan.

"He was truly lucky. It [the bullet] hit his hip and was apparently nearly spent since it didn't shatter the hip but rode around it and came out in front. When the telegram came our 5 year old daughter was crying with me, and finally when things calmed down she said 'Momma, what is wounded?' She didn't know why we were crying."

He was in Japan for some time—I can't recall how long—but recovered, and was sent on my birthday, Nov. 25, 1950, in time to go to Chosin. What a lovely birthday gift! I met a chaplain who had been with my husband when he was wounded. He was amazed to hear George had been sent back to Korea.

I drove to Florida with my little girl to visit my family and an old school chum whose husband was also away in the Marines. Also made a brief trip to Philadelphia with a young neighbor—a sergeant's wife who wanted to go home and was afraid to travel alone. My daughter and I returned by bus. Our bus arrived at Lejeune at midnight. I was so pleased with my decision to leave my car at the base bus station. Was able to just hop in and drove home. I had notified the MP's. They said it was a good thing I did, or they would have towed the car away.

Carole and Connie.

Christmas, Lejeune.

Christmas 1950. Still smiling!

BILLYE JO HARVEY

I was born Billye Jo Harvey to C. E. and Eula Key Harvey on 1 September 1929 in Kaufman, Texas. My mother swore it was the hottest day on record; as my mother never swore, it must have been true. Due to my baby brother's death, I was raised an only child.

Kaufman was a town of three thousand, just thirty miles southeast of Dallas. Everyone knew everyone; if you misbehaved, word was soon back to your family. It was a lovely little town with big trees and flowers, a big courthouse with stores all around the square. No one locked their doors or cars—if they were lucky enough to have one. The only air-conditioning we knew was at the Saturday-afternoon cowboy movie, but we knew all about fans—hand as well as electric. We had one radio and one operator-assisted telephone as our link to the outside world. And don't forget the penny postcard!

It was a great place and time to be a little girl. I played in my father's lumberyard, helped the black woman wash the clothes outside over a fire under the big washpot, took a bath under the honeysuckle arbor to be cool, went crawdad fishing, played rubber guns with the boys and dolls with the girls. We didn't know that we were poor, had little cash, and *depression* was just a big word.

When the war came, I was in high school, taking piano lessons, entering declamation contests, marching as a drum majorette, and helping my mother bake cakes that she sold. We began having dances in some of the homes, having dates, and playing Spin the Bottle and Post Office. Then this new boy moved to town, and things were never the same again.

Jack L. Nolan was like a breath of fresh air. His life had been as different from ours as day and night. His mother died when he was two, his father when he was nine, and then he was pushed from one relative to another until, finally, there was no one but his oldest sister, Catherine. She and her husband took the responsibility, and Jack had a home.

He joined our little class of thirty-four our junior year, and we began dating. Now this meant walking to school together, playing cards, listening to records, or making fudge at someone's house. There were no cars, no tires, no gas; Crisco came in jars, oleo was white, and we had ration stamps for shoes and meat. But we had a good time.

At the end of our senior year, Jack had been football captain, and I was voted most favorite girl in school. We were in love. Most of us were going on to college, but Jack could see that he was again on his own. He studied the situation and rode a bus to Dallas to join the United States Marine Corps on 26 July 1946. He wouldn't be eighteen until 13 August.

During the first years of college, Jack and I wrote to each other and dated other people and went on with our learning and living. When he flew in from Quantico the Christmas of 1948 in his dress blues and gold bars, I was certain that I had never seen anything so wonderful. I decided then that he was the *one* for me, and fortunately, he felt the same about me.

The college years were fun, and I enjoyed them. Lubbock was a long way from Kaufman, but I got home often enough. I dated while writing Jack long letters and looking at his photo. I was in the rodeo parades (had to get the handmade boots and do the "sugar-water cured hat" bit). I worked as a student assistant and modeled. I also elected to go for the grades and have enough of an ego that I enjoyed looking at the senior annual and seeing the honors that I accrued. Then Jack arrived for my graduation from Texas Technological University on May 1950, and love was wonderful.

Billye Harvey in Texas Tech, modeling shot.

Billye Harvey with Texas Tech roommate, 1948.

Billye Harvey and Mom, Easter 1947.

Jack Nolan in Bougainville, World War II.

BILLYE HARVEY NOLAN

TYLER TX
21 SEPTEMBER 1991

MY 1950 EXPERIENCE

Location at outbreak? On honeymoon somewhere between Texas and California. Jack had received a forty-five-day leave; he came to Lubbock for my graduation from Texas Tech University on 28 May 1950. I must add that having the tall, uniformed marine calling at the dorm did cause a mild sensation. We were married in Kaufman,Texas, on 10 June 1950. We began our trip back to Camp Pendleton in a new Ford (un-air-conditioned, of course), but we did have a wonderful time. We were not listening to news reports and didn't even know about Korea until the Saturday he reported in and was restricted to base. Then life turned upside down!

It was certainly difficult being newlyweds and preparing for war at the same time. Jack would be in San Diego, loading the USS *George Clymer,* and would come in at all hours of the night. We said good-bye several times as we never knew if he would be back that night or not. During this time, I met some of the marines and their wives. Some of them, we have remained friends and keep in touch all this time; some, we have just lost contact over the years. I especially remember the big brigade parade. We were due to attend the reception afterward, but Jack and Nick came to the car where Dottie and I were and told us to forget the reception—big party. And it really was. Four bachelors shared a house in Oceanside and were hosts. After being introduced to the Bird Game, I still have a slight headache from that evening.

I was twenty. Jack left thirty-four days after our wedding. We were staying in Sterling Housing in Oceanside, California. He had sublet a one-bedroom apartment. They left us a lot of C-rations, which Kenny loves to laugh about to this day. But they did have a wringer washing machine!

So Jack sailed away and left me in Oceanside, not knowing but a few marine wives, with a new car (but I could not drive), and unknown to me, pregnant. This was my introduction to the USMC; thank goodness things did get better later. But I still think that Jack hated to leave the new car more than he hated to leave me. Before we married, he told me that the USMC was first in his life. That was hard to accept, but now I understand. What really hurt was to be number 3—USMC, new car, and then me, the young, innocent bride.

Our financial circumstances were fine; he quickly got an allotment set up for me and had a full power of attorney drawn (which is still in effect).

When I realized I was pregnant and so sick I could not hold my head up and had to move from Sterling, I got an apartment on the beach. It was a terrible time. I was so nauseated I couldn't eat and didn't want to get out of bed. The war news was not good; Jack was wounded on 6 Aug. He called me from Japan before I was notified by the USMC. Then his picture came out in *Life,* and I didn't recognize him with the mustache. Trying to learn how to drive and to write the wedding thank-you notes was just a nightmare. If I had not been so ill, I believe that I could have coped better. I really did not want to be pregnant that soon after marriage, but life has a way of going its own way—I was definitely not in control.

It was decided that the best thing for me to do was to go back to Texas. My parents, C. E. and Eula Harvey, drove a car (to be transported) to California and packed my few things and me into the new black Ford. I will say that it was a wonderful relief to have them there to take over; I'm not real sure just how they felt. They had just married me off, and three months later, they had me back. But I needed help, and bless their hearts, they were there to give it. We began the trek to Texas. At least we came a different way. They wanted to see the Grand Canyon and Hoover Dam. While touring the dam, my mother found a five-dollar bill. She begged my father to take us back to Las Vegas to play the five dollars (knowing her, she would have parlayed it into bigger winnings). But my dad was too much of a Baptist for that, so she bought supper. I lay in the backseat and thought I was going to die. It was a terrible way to come home.

But coming back to Kaufman was the best thing for me—actually, for all of us. Jack's sister and brother-in-law, Catherine and Guy Shaw, who raised him since he was thirteen years old, had their own clinic and hospital. He was Dr. Shaw, and she was his nurse; his mother was the receptionist. I was home!

I moved into my old room, helped my mother in her jewelry store, saw all my old friends, and began feeling better. I did think that I might live. I suffered some surprise when my mother said that now that I had an income, I should pay room and board. She was right, and I did as that USMC allotment never missed coming to our little bank there. It wasn't much, but it was something. I even did the driving and passed the test on my first try.

In October of 1950, Jack was out of the hospital in Japan and had rejoined his outfit. He resumed his old job as a platoon leader in E-2-5. He was great about writing. I would get several letters at a time, then go for days before the next batch. But it didn't matter; they were like gold. His Thanksgiving letter was especially jubilant. They had enjoyed a gourmet meal, and McArthur had announced that the troops would be home by Christmas. Life was beginning to be beautiful again.

The Chinese took care of that. We began hearing some bad news about the marines, the cold, the enemy hordes, and Chosin. The newspapers, *Life*, and the radio (no TV then) reports were all *bad*. It was a terrible time, and I felt as if I were living from day to day. My last letter had been the Thanksgiving Day one, and I was frantic. One day just before Christmas, I was in the jewelry store, working, and got a call from the post office that I had a letter. Even though mail was delivered twice a day to the store, everyone in town was waiting for me to hear. I ran the two blocks to the PO for that precious piece of paper. Jack was alive and well. I could breathe again.

He was the first one back from the war from the Dallas area. I had received a letter in late March of 1951 from the *Dallas Morning News*, requesting an interview upon his return. He called from California, saying that his flight would be in on Sunday, 25 March 1951. Guy would not let me go to Dallas to meet the plane; in fact, I went into the hospital, and that's where I was when he came home. Baby took some time to come. But the newspaper didn't. So while I was in labor, he was being interviewed and photographed. Finally, at about 8:00 p.m. on Monday, 26 March 1951, our daughter, Nina, was born.

Tuesday's edition had a full front-page picture and write-up of 2nd Lt. Jack L. Nolan and his experiences. It also said his wife was in labor; my name was never mentioned, and to this day, I am angry. It was a great write-up, and he spoke to several service clubs before we three packed into the little black Ford and headed back to Camp Pendleton in California. Need I say this journey was quite different from the one so blissfully traveled ten months before?

Billye and Jack, 1946.

The Dallas Morning News brings the world to your doorstep, with news, comics, features, and opinions, for a few pennies each day.

The Dallas M

Oldest Business Institution in Texas—Founded in Galveston, Apr

66TH YEAR IN DALLAS DALLAS, TEXAS, TUESDAY, MARCH 27, 1951 — 4

—Dallas News Staff Photo by Clint Grant.

KOREA VETERAN SWEATS IT OUT

Lt. Jack L. Nolan of Kaufman returned from Korea Sunday to sweat out the arrival of his first child. He got a little help from a nephew, Robert Shaw, 3, who offered to wipe his brow.

150 Marines From Texas On Way Home

SAN FRANCISCO, Calif., March 20 (AP).—Almost 150 Texans are among the 1,500 United States Marines returning home this week on rotation after seven months' action in Korea.

They are on the U.S.S. Gen. G. M. Randall, due here Thursday.

Among Marines of the Dallas area en route home are:

Cpl. Stephen H. Armstrong, Fort Worth; Sgt. Welton W. Atchison, Waco; S Sgt. Robert L. Ben, Mexia; Pfc. Rayburn L. Blair, Arlington; Sgt. Norris G. Blankenship, Marl; T Sgt. Truman G. Bunee, Kilgore; Maj. Albert L. Clark, Longview; Pfc. Duel D. Crabb, Fort Worth.

Sgt. Ralph O. Duncan, 2711 Fielder Court, Dallas; Pfc. Bryon T. Ellis, Tyler; T/Sgt. Felix G. Ezell, Greenville; T Sgt. Charles O. Goddard, Route 7, Palestine; Cpl. Joe S. Gordon, 2648 Richmond Avenue, Dallas; Cpl. Delbert Griffin, Sulphur Springs; Sgt. Billy J. Guessen, Ponder; Second Lt. James E. Harrell, Waco; Cpl. John T. Johnson, Waco; Pfc. Willard A. Jones, Longview; Pfc. Billy C. Kelley, Longview.

Capt. John B. Long, Fort Worth; Cpl. Francisco Lopes Jr., Fort Worth; Cpl. Doyle R. Mitchell, 1415½ Pennsylvania Avenue, Dallas; Sgt. Herman Mullines, Van Alstyne; Pfc. Marvin Munchrath, 327 Francis, Dallas; Cpl. Leonard H. Nolan, Route 2, Box 37, Dallas.

Second Lt. Jack L. Nolan, Kaufman; Pfc. Gordon L. Phillips, 2900 Comer, Dallas; Cpl. Drewry A. Prater, 3708 Corlett, Dallas; Sgt. Clarence F. Prince, 3117 Westminster, Dallas; Sgt. Murrell W. Reynolds, Mount Vernon.

Cpl. James M. Selby, 3111 Birmingham, Dallas; Pfc. Billy C. Smith, Irving; Pfc. Charles Y. Smith, Fort Worth; Sgt. Richard L. Trahan, Lufkin; Sgt. William R. Tuck, Texarkana; Sgt. Erwin G. Van Sickle, Greenville; Sgt. Arthur C. Wolters Jr., Lewisville; Sgt. Sammie F. Wright, Fort Worth.

Nobody Wins Korea War,

"But that's big, wild country where we make one move and they make another, as in chess."

"All we can do," he said, "is kill so many Chinese soldiers that the Communists will wish they'd never ...

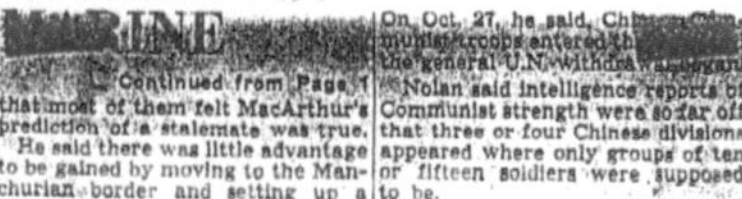

...RINE

Continued from Page 1

that most of them felt MacArthur's prediction of a stalemate was true.

He said there was little advantage to be gained by moving to the Manchurian border and setting up a

On Oct. 27, he said, Chi... munist troops entered th... the general U.N. withdra...

Nolan said intelligence reports of Communist strength were so far off that three or four Chinese divisions appeared where only groups of ten or fifteen soldiers were supposed to be.

DALLAS, TEXAS, TUESDAY, MARCH 27, 1951
—Dallas News Staff Photo by Clint Grant.

KOREA VETERAN SWEATS IT OUT

Lt. Jack L. Nolan of Kaufman returned from Korea Sunday to sweat out the arrival of his first child. He got a little help from a nephew, Robert Shaw, 3, who offered to wipe his brow.

...rning News

PART 1

, 1842—Established in Dallas, October 1, 188...

'AGES IN 3 PARTS — PRICE 5 CENTS

NO. 178

...A GIRL

First Baby Greets Veteran of Korea

Special to The News.

KAUFMAN, Texas, March 27.—The long sweat was over Thursday for Lt. Jack L. Nolan.

A day after he returned from eight months in Korea, the Kaufman Marine officer's wife delivered a 7-pound, 5 ounce baby girl.

Nolan, a combat officer in the first Marine unit to reach Korea [illegible]gust, arrived in San Fran[illegible]ursday, then flew to Dallas Easter afternoon. His wife failed to meet him at Love Field because she had entered the hospital Sunday morning to have their first child.

The baby, a girl named Nina, arrived more than thirty-six hours after Mrs. Nolan went to the hospital.

The 23-year-old Marine, whose Purple Heart gave him priority on the Marine rotation list, had a pointed comment: "Whew!"

Reprinted with permission of the Dallas Morning News.

The paper had written me a letter asking about Jack's return. He responded; this was the result. But they never put my *name* in it . . . just "his wife"!

This was *Dallas News*, dated Wednesday, March 28, 1951.

First Baby Greets Veteran of Korea

Special to The News

KAUFMAN, Texas, March 27—The long sweat was over Thursday for Lt. Jack L. Nolan.

A day after he returned from eight months in Korea, the Kaufman Marine officer's wife delivered a 7-pound, 5 ounce baby girl.

Nolan, a combat officer in the first Marine unit to reach Korea ??? arrived in San Francisco ??? Thursday, then flew to Dallas Easter afternoon. His wife failed to meet him at Love Field because she had entered the hospital Sunday morning to have their first child.

The baby, a girl named Nina, arrived more than thirty-six hours after Mrs. Nolan went to the hospital.

The 23-year-old Marine, whose Purple Heart gave him priority on the Marine rotation list, had a pointed comment:

'Whew!'

LOIS MITCHELL

Joe and I were married on June 9, 1948, in Holland, Michigan. We soon found ourselves living in an apartment in downtown Quantico, Virginia, a far cry from my expectations as a young wife of one of our future marine generals (as all our men were told, remember?)

A year later, we were given quarters in Midway Village, only to move again into converted-barracks housing in Whiskey Gulch. We were at the bottom of the hill from Waller Hall and the O club. It was an ideal spot for all our friends to drop by when leaving the club. Many of them needed a strong cup of coffee and some breakfast as well.

Joe received his orders for Korea in May of 1952. By then, we were the parents of a three-year-old daughter and a sixteen-month-old son. We left our comfortable quarters, and the children and I settled into a small apartment in Holland. This was my home, and I chose to move back to be near my parents and seven brothers and sisters. I had a lot of caring family and friends to help me, and being so young, I was glad to be home. As military wives, though, we all knew no one could ever fill the lonely times we felt without our marine.

At the time Joe left, I did not even drive. I was left with a brand-new car and two babies to transport around, so I soon learned! It was quite an experience, driving in the Michigan winter. Living in a civilian community again was quite different. There were acquaintances who asked, 'Where is Korea?' 'Why is Joe there?' and 'Why can't you and the children be with him?' We knew, even then, Korea would be the Forgotten War.

Joe's letters came about once a week, and then I heard nothing for weeks. I knew something was wrong, and the waiting was so hard. His next letter finally did arrive, and he explained he had been in a military ambush situation, for which he later received the Silver Star. Thank God he was okay; I was so proud of him! Our hometown paper, however, created a little amusement for Joe and all of us. It stated, 'Husband of Local Woman Awarded Silver Star.' Joe had to share the headline with his wife!

I have always felt I made the right choice, coming home to live. I had companionships, security, no financial problems, and the love of family and friends. Not all wives had the choice I had, and I'm sure they may have endured more hardships than I did. Still, it was a hard year or more for all of us.

Little did we know then . . . there would be many more separations from our career marine.

Second Lt. Joseph P. Mitchell and commanding officers.

Second Lt. Joseph P. Mitchell of Holland, Michigan, receives the Silver Star Medal for gallantry and intrepidity in action from his regimental commander.

Lois Mitchell with the couple's children: daughter, Paula, and son, Darryl.

Corpus Christi, TX
April 8, 1998

From The Desk Of: Mary Jane Sullivan, Ph.D.
Licensed Consulting Psychologist (Ret.)

Biographical Sketch Prior to Marriage:

"Born November 9, 1928, Gary, Indiana. First generation Sicilian [and damned proud of it] (an' ifa yu don'a like it, I'll hav' me goombodies in the Mafia talka you 'bout it [VBG]). Various grade schools. High School Lew Wallace. Sophomore Class VP, Junior Class Treasurer, Senior Honor Society, top 10% of the class academically. Graduated June, 1946. Attended Indiana University, Bloomington, for freshman year. Moved to California with family. Attended Pasadena JC for one semester. Moved back to Indiana with family in November, '47. Became engaged to SSgt R. E. Sullivan, December, '47. Sully would be the first non-Sicilian to enter the family, and I the first first-generation person to enter his. This was taken very seriously in Gary, Indiana at that time. (Had known each other since I was 12 and Sully was 13.) Sully was stationed on Guam at time of engagement, then extended in the Corps and Overseas for reassignment to Tsingtao, China. Was contemplating joining him there and being married in China when his commission and assignment to 5th Basic Class came through. We were married on 28 December, 1948 with 2nd Lt. R.D. Newmann, complete with 'Boat Cape, as Best Man.'"

Mary Jane and Ralph Sullivan were living in Sterling Housing with their nine-month-old daughter, Jane Marie, when they first got news of the Korean War outbreak. Mary Jane was twenty-one and had been married a year and a half. Separation was not new for her. Ralph had been deployed for several months. The outfit he commanded was not in the brigade, so it appeared Korea would not involve him. However, he was transferred to D-2-5, and his trip to Korea was assured.

Shortly after our engagement in 1947.

"My seventeen year old sister was visiting with us when Sully left. My parents, who lived in Gary, Indiana, sent my 19 year old brother out to California to drive us home, since neither I nor my sister drove. When we got back home, my daughter and I lived with my parents.

Sully's parents lived just a block away. In short, my living conditions were excellent, and my support systems totally intact. I know that this was very different from the experiences of many of my peer group. Things would become tough enough without having to face the situation alone."

"Sully must have drawn a 'dead horse' so that I had money to get along on. We certainly had no savings, but had a car and furniture payments. Oh—just remembered we were still making uniform payments, too. Fortunately, Sully was able to cancel the order for his sword before he left, or I'd have been stuck with making payments for that useless piece of gear, too."

"Sully was wounded twice with the Brigade (August 7th, GSW to the head and August 10th, wounds, multiple, extreme) and once with the Division (September 23d, wound, fragment, left lower leg.) What made all this difficult was the fact that the mail situation never did get straightened out. An article appearing in the 'Chicago Tribune' by Keyes Beech suggested that Sully had been reported as KIA, and that the battalion had been surprised when he turned up on the radio. A wife, who was living a short distance away in Chicago Heights (the wife of a 2nd Lt. Tank Officer, also with the Brigade) saw the article and drove over to make me aware. Then the telegrams began to arrive: The first, MIA; the second, KIA, body not recovered; then two in rapid succession 'WIA.' Then we got a letter from Sully, written from the Danish hospital ship 'Jutlandia' en route to Japan, bringing us up to date. Sully left July 14th and returned on our anniversary, December 28th."

Mary Jane was helped through this time by being with family. She had already endured a six-month hardship tour prior to Korea when Sully was on TDY from October '49 to March '50.

"He was swanning around off Hawaii and in the Bering Sea with Recon Company while the wives were literally starving to death on the beach. Because he was on TDY rather than POC, he could not draw a dead horse. He and the rest of the people from Recon and A

Co. 7th sat aboard their submarines and APDS with pockets full of money but unable to get to a post office to mail it home. I, and many others that I could name, were literally down to our last handful of beans when their ships returned to San Diego. We were, after all, the wives of Marine officers, and we wouldn't go to Navy Relief, the Red Cross, or anyone else to get help. We were too proud."

Jane, our daughter, and I, taken while Sully was in Korea, 1950.

Jane and I at my parents',
where we lived while he was in Korea

Sully, Jane, and I at Sterling Housing prior to his embarkation to Korea.

Jane and I at Homoja Housing in early 1950.

Sully loading Jane in a seabag prior to leaving for Korea.

Shades of Homoja and living in one-half of a Quonset hut.

Sully and I upon his return from Korea.

CAROLINE and **BILL SCHREIER** met when they were members in a friend's wedding. The year was 1947. Bill and the groom were marine pilots stationed at Cherry Point, North Carolina. Caroline lived in New Bern, North Carolina, so she was acquainted with the marines and the military. Her father owned a lumber mill, and her family had lived for three generations in New Bern. Caroline and Bill were married in 1949 as soon as she graduated from college with her degree in education.

When the Korean War broke out, they were stationed at Camp Lejeune, North Carolina, and had been married a little over a year. She was twenty-two and in the hospital with a new baby, William Jr., when she heard marines were being sent to fight. Bill left with the Fifth Marines when the baby was seven weeks old. Caroline found out that the movers were not going to get around to her for three weeks. Her father and some men from his mill came to her rescue, and she and the baby were moved back to New Bern. They spent their separation from Bill with her parents. After seven months of fighting, he was wounded and sent back. The family was reunited.

HENRIETTA "BOOTS" HANSEN had a brand-new daughter born July 10 in the evening, just hours before the new father, Dean Hansen, shipped out with the First Marine Brigade to Korea. They had known he was leaving since late June. They were living in Oceanside, California. while Dean was stationed at Camp Pendleton. Boots was twenty-five. The Hansens had been married two years. It would be easier with a new baby to be at home with family in Wisconsin. Boots waited there for Dean. They were separated six months. He was wounded and sent home.

MARGERY and **JIM RITCHART** were high school sweethearts in Vinton, Iowa. Marge worked at a bank. Jim's dreams were to become a highway patrolman, but he was too young. Instead, he enlisted in the Marine Corps until he became twenty-two and old enough to join the highway patrol. He was soon to find he wasn't too old for combat and violence beyond anything he would see on our highways.

Marge and Jim were married after boot camp, and three months later, he left for Camp Pendleton and points farther east—Korea. Marge was nineteen and expecting their first child. They were living on a PFC's pay and broke. They didn't have enough money for a car, just about $300 that Marge had managed to save while working at the bank. There was no reason for Marge to follow Jim to the West Coast. It was better for her to stay behind with their families. During their separation, Marge lived with her parents or Jim's mother. The families were very supportive during this difficult time.

Jim was wounded in action at Seoul, but he rejoined his outfit and took part in the action at the Chosin Reservoir. At the time, their son was born. Marge didn't know whether Jim was alive or dead. After that first scare when he was wounded, each letter meant he was all right—then—but there was always a question mark. Was he still okay? The war ended for him when he was evacuated with frostbite. He returned to Vinton, decorated.

Marge and Jim were reunited. The baby was five months old when his daddy first saw him. Jim returned for duty at Pendleton, and Marge and little Allen were able to join him there.

WINONA SMELT married her marine when he came home at the end of World War II. They had been married four years when the Korean War broke out. This was not a new scenario for them. He was expected to deploy.

The couple was on vacation in Washington and Oregon. When they returned to California, they got the news that her husband's engineer battalion and the brigade were shipping out for Korea. The next few weeks were a frenzy of activity. The men were loading ships day and night. It caught Winona by surprise, but she felt her husband had been keeping up with events in that faraway place.

They had lived in base housing, Sterling, and Homoja. Then they found a place in Escondido. It meant a drive, but it gave them privacy. This is where Winona stayed when her husband shipped out. He was on temporary orders, so there were no funds for her to relocate. Also, they hoped when he came home, he would be reassigned to the same base, Camp Pendleton. That wasn't to happen, but after all, that was the Marine Corps.

Winona and her baby daughter, Ruthie, waited ten months for their part of the war to be over. It was not a particularly difficult time. There wasn't very much money, but they did have a car. An accident ended his stint in Korea. He was hit by a truck on the march back from the Chosin. The family was reunited, but it took awhile before Ruthie would accept this man as her father.

ELEANOR CARMICHAEL

"I always say, 'If you are going to worry, wait till you have something to worry about.'" That's Eleanor Carmichael's philosophy, and it stood her in good stead. She met her marine at 8th and I (Headquarters, Marine Corps) in Washington, DC. They had been married eleven years by the time the Korean War broke out. After World War II, war was an old acquaintance. She and her husband got to California in February and were living in Homoja Government Housing with their seven-year-old daughter. This was Eleanor's first move as a wife. She was twenty-five and had been working while they lived in Washington.

In July the news came that the brigade was being deployed. Her husband volunteered and would become a member of the Chosin Few. After he left, Eleanor returned to her home in DC. She drove with her daughter and two other wives who needed rides back across the country. One was the young wife of a PFC—dead broke and seven months pregnant. Eleanor drove all the way.

At her return to DC, she moved back in her house, where her mother was living. Eleanor got a temporary job as a waitress so she could rejoin her husband when he returned. She listened to the dark news reports but refused to believe them. She knew her husband was all right. He had contracted malaria in World War II but came through the Korean conflict safely.

PAT LENNON stayed at her parents' home in a city in the center of the United States—one as American as apple pie—but her friends and neighbors couldn't comprehend why she was by herself or why her husband was in Korea. "Where's your husband?" "Why are you back home?" She and Tom hadn't even celebrated their second wedding anniversary when he was deployed along with his fellow marines to a small spot around the world. Pat was in the first months of a difficult pregnancy, and this didn't make the separation any easier.

This was Pat's third pregnancy. She had been pregnant twice before, both of which ended in miscarriages. At two months along, Pat was in bed, trying to carry this one to full term. She found out Tom was leaving when he came home from the big Fourth of July parade with the news that he would be leaving in a few weeks with the brigade.

It seemed the expedient thing for Pat was to go home to her parents in Kansas City. She was unable to handle the packing and the move from the apartment in Sterling Housing, so a neighbor couple packed up the contents of the one bedroom for them. The Lennons' big boxer dog was crated up for his trip to his new home. The car was sold by a relative. This gave Pat money to live on until Tom returned home.

Tom was wounded at the Pusan Perimeter. He was in the hospital in Japan for an extended time, then at Tripler Army Hospital in Honolulu, and finally sent to the military hospital outside Memphis.

Pat was out of bed and able to join him for a visit after Christmas. They had a small one-bedroom apartment that soon became more crowded when little Tommy decided it was time for him to arrive on the scene. To the surprise of everyone, doctors and nurses included, he was born on January 17—a full month early—all five pounds, eight ounces of healthy, colicky baby boy!

Tom and Pat had a room across from each other in the hospital. Mother and baby beat Dad home. They left the hospital after two days. Pat's mother came down with baby clothes and stayed for a few days.

Life for the Lennon family returned to normal, but the next time the US government saw fit to separate them, Pat stayed with her marine buddies at Camp Pendleton because, at least, they understood.

LOUISE SCHRYVER (MRS. HUGH)

The summer of 1950 found Second Lieutenant and Mrs. Schryver at Camp Pendleton, awaiting the birth of their second child. By the first of July, Hugh "Nick" Schryver got orders to ship out to Korea with his unit, B Co. 1/5. The Schryvers were living in Homoja Housing Project with their son, who was at that time one year and four months. Louise Schryver was twenty-one. They had been married two years and two months.

The brigade shipped out, and the very next day, July 15, their daughter was born. Louise was faced with going home from the hospital with a brand-new baby and having to pack and move. Money was tight. Fortunately, her mother was able to come from Corpus Christi, Texas, and handle the move back home to Texas. They returned on the train. The Schryvers had a car, but Louise couldn't drive. Her brother came down and took the car back with him.

Nick was gone eight months. He was wounded. Louise and her babies lived with her parents until Nick came home.

Louise's comment on the experience: "The Marine Corps was our husband's occupation. We had to accept the fact he had to deploy."

WINIFRED "WYN" VAN CLEVE KELLEY

BELTON, TX

Dear Adrienne,

It was so nice to have your letter and thank you for your caring. It has indeed been a most difficult time. I do plan to leave about June 9th and drive to West Virginia to visit my brother and family. My brother is a medical doctor, a minister, a poet, and is a peck of fun. That should help a lot. Then I am going to Waynesboro, Va. for a visit with Roy's sister and family. The first week of July, Roy's sister, husband, their 5 sons and their wives, and NINE children and THIS PERSON are going to the beach on the outer banks of N.C. for a week. Should be very interesting.

Enough of that!! I will try to answer your questionnaire. Roy's time in Korea was very short. After Basic School and a summer of instructing, Roy was assigned to the First Platoon, Company G, 3rd Battalion 6th Marines. In May of 1950, that Battalion was sent to the Mediterranean for the 6 month cruise. I was living in Holly Ridge with our 4 month old son. On a Friday in July, I was told to check back on Monday to be assigned quarters on the base at Camp Lejeune—sure I would! When I checked back on Monday, I was informed that the 3rd Battalion 6th Marines had been detached from the 6th Fleet and sent to Japan for assignment to Korea. Also, I was told that I had to vacate 'quarters' at Holly Ridge—which I didn't do.

Roy was assigned to the First Platoon, Company G, Third Battalion, Seventh Marines which was then sent to Seoul, Korea. I think that was sometime in September shortly after THE Inchon landing. Roy lasted 8 days before he was wounded and evacuated to the hospital in Yokosuka. He was in the hospital there for 2 months and then sent back to the US. Tho his wound was not life threatening, it disabled his right arm—which was not compatible with firing a rifle or pistol.

The only amusing thing I can relate is: After Roy was wounded and on a stretcher, the nurse asked him the name and address of the next of kin. Roy replied that his next of kin was his wife, Winifred Van Cleve, The Beta House, Centre College, Danville, Kentucky. The nurse raised her eyebrows, but said no more then. The next morning, she came back and said she must have misunderstood him. Would he please give her the name and address of his next of kin. Roy repeated what he had told her the night before. The nurse said, 'But, Sir, that is a fraternity house.' Roy said, 'I know.' She left shaking her head. When Roy was being 'loaded' aboard ship for evacuation to Japan, he saw the nurse and beckoned to her to come over to him. He said, 'I don't know where my wife is right now, but her mother is the house mother for the Beta Theta Phi Fraternity at Centre College.' I think she was greatly relieved and perhaps my reputation was saved. My father had died of a massive coronary in March, 1950, and my brother's fraternity brothers had come to the funeral. They had just lost their housemother and had asked my mother to be their house mother. That was a Godsend for her.

Roy was in the hospital in Japan for 2 months then sent back to the States in time for Christmas and our son's first birthday—which IS Christmas day. I had left Holly Ridge in late November and was at that time staying at the Beta House since it was Christmas vacation by the time I got there.

I know this isn't very interesting or exciting, but that's the way it was. I do wish you the best of luck with your endeavor. I KNOW how much work it is, but also how much you will enjoy doing it

I hope to see you both sometime this fall.

Love,
Wyn Van Cleve Kelley

JOYCE STUART

(MRS. VAUGHN)

On July 2, Joyce and Vaughn Stuart got married. That was 1948 and right after Joyce graduated from high school. She was seventeen. In July 1950, they celebrated their second wedding anniversary just before Vaughn was deployed with the brigade to Korea. They had no children.

Joyce and Vaughn were living in Sterling Housing, a complex of two-story apartment buildings, when the war broke out. Joyce had to move out of the apartment. She and her sister lived together in El Monte, California, until Vaughn came home. During this time Joyce worked for Bank of America. They didn't have a car, so she depended on the streetcar for transportation.

Vaughn was wounded in the eyes and face. They were separated for a year.

JEANNE M. STEMPLE

Jim and I were stationed at Camp Lejeune when the Korean War broke out. We were living in a charming almost-new cottage at Wrightsville Beach across the street from the ocean. Our rent was $50 a month and a struggle to pay on a second lieutenant's salary. Our landlords were a prominent local dentist and his wife who took us under their wings and became very good friends. Several of Jim's classmates and their families lived nearby—Mae and Marv, Cora and Gene, and Maida and Bill, just down the street—so we had lots of company. The cottage only had one oil heater for the entire house, which was located in the living/dining area, and we lived in fear of it blowing up one day. To our horror, it happened one evening while we were at the movies.

As the summer months approached, we knew we would have to find another place to live as the rent on our cottage would double. It was welcome news when our landlord said he would convert his basement into a summer apartment for us at a price we could afford. There was just one catch—Jim would have to help him with the conversion in the evenings and on the weekends. By this time, I was expecting our first child, and not a day went by that I wasn't deathly ill. When Jim's orders came through to leave for Korea, it was 'pack up and leave tomorrow.' We had very few household goods, so my parents arranged for a family friend to come to Wrightsville Beach and pack everything into our old Chevy and drive the car back to my hometown, Pennington, New Jersey, where I would stay with my parents until, and if, Jim came home. It was a terrible, traumatic time for both of us.

Jim returned to the States in late December, just in time for the birth of our daughter, Linda, on Christmas Eve 1950. He was sent to St. Albans Naval Hospital on Long Island to be treated with a new medication for frostbite contracted at the Chosin Reservoir. He was very fortunate as this was the only hospital that successfully treated this condition, thus avoiding amputation. When Jim recovered, we gathered our family together and moved to New York, where Jim was now stationed at the Brooklyn Navy Yard, an interesting and enjoyable tour for all of us.

by Jeanne M. Stemple

META J. REED

Hot Springs, AR
June 18, 1997

Dear Adrienne:

You have started on a very ambitious project and I wish you well. Here are a few of my memories from that time in our life

In May of 1950 Jack was a lieutenant assigned to Force ANGLICO at Camp Lejeune. Of course we didn't have quarters and had left a room with kitchen privileges in New Bern for a two room apartment with small bath, across from a junk yard, in Jacksonville. We had been married for three and a half years. Mac and Bev lived in the other half of this little house. Caroline and Bill Schreier were across the street. The commute from New Bern to Lejeune had been a bummer. Jack seemed to 'leave in the dark and come home in the dark' In May, Jack and others, received orders to Pensacola for *refresher* flight training so we were busy getting ready to leave when the Korean War started. We had just returned from leave and were at the Onslow Beach Club and heard the news that the North Koreans had invaded

South Korea. We had a vague idea of where Korea was. Little did we realize the impact that this far away country was going to have on us. Of course the 2nd Division was adither and everyone was wondering what was going to happen next.

My comfort level was pretty good as we were leaving. I felt that this coming war was not going to affect me, at least not immediately. Everyone seemed to think that it would be over in a few weeks.

The next day Jack went to the base to pick up his orders. It was easy going in . . . coming out was a different story. Only three people were allowed to leave the base and Jack didn't have stars on his collar. He got word to me that there was some foul up and it was going to take a bit of time to sort it out. It took the entire day to convince those in charge that he did have orders in hand and was to report to Pensacola. Seems that there was something about a critical MOS. Finally he was released to carry out his orders. During my personal 'longest day,' I sat on the front steps of an empty apartment, waiting and wondering. Our meager household effects had already gone and all we had was the 'two parachute bags, pots and pans and a toaster.'

Jack finally arrived home late in the afternoon. We had some supper someplace and went to friends that evening. The unit had their orders and boxes had been left so they could pack and move. We helped with the packing by cleaning out the Liquor Locker, after all, liquor was a 'no-no' in household effects. The dregs in all the bottles when mixed together make a wicked brew!

On Tuesday morning, Jack and I and the loaded-down Chevy left for Pensacola. Even then the trains were pulling into Camp Lejeune as the division prepared to move out.

Some were already in Pensacola and had lined up a temporary place to stay while we looked for more adequate housing. Refresher flight training began right after the 4th of July, and Jack was back into the 'up in the dark, home in the dark' routine. A friend and her girls were my salvation. In December, Jack and Bill had to pack up and go to Corpus Christi for advanced training. I stayed in Pensacola as he wasn't supposed to be gone long. In January my first crisis arrived in the form of a 'blue norther,' Florida style. My pipes froze, my bathroom froze, my shower was a shambles along with the kitchen stuff, and here came 'Jolly Jack' flying in from Corpus for a nice weekend. He went back, and my pipes thawed out. I became very interested in plumbers at that point.

In March, refresher training was over, and orders arrived—the ones that most of the wives of the 5th Basic had already suffered, and now it was my turn. I know I wasn't the only one in the world in the same situation, but I thought I was. Jack was going to MCAS El Toro and after work-up training would be going to Korea with the 13th replacement draft. That number 13 sort of go to me. That meant that on September 16th, 1951 it was my guy's turn . . .

We decided that our short tour at El Toro would be as good as we could make it and not look to the future for we both believed it was just another absence . . .

absences that I had come to tolerate but to which I would never become accustomed . . .

Time flew. Our finances looked pretty good, the car was fairly new, and going home to Iowa seemed the logical step. We had our second honeymoon at Big Sur and San Francisco and returned to El Toro. Jack's parents came to see my husband and their son off and drive me back to Iowa.

Without children it was easy for me to move in with Jack's parents at the lake, and also I was only an hour or so away from my parents and brother. Family was very important to me at this time.

I lived in Solon, Iowa, which is between Iowa City and Cedar Rapids. Feeling that I had to do something besides write letters to strange addresses full of cryptic acronyms and numbers, I went to work. My secretarial skills found me a job with Collins Radio in Cedar Rapids, some 22 miles from Solon. Now it was my turn to be 'up in the dark, home in the dark.' Jack's letters began to flow in on an almost daily basis, telling of the flights over Korea, the country, the people, the tent, the squadron, and all those things men talk about. He was based at K-1 and K-18 and flying almost every day. I was acquiring a whole new military lexicon. One of the hardest things for me to do was to think of things to send him. Eats, puzzles, books seemed to work, but the ukulele I sent scored the biggest hit although his tent mates must have become pretty tired of 'my dog has fleas.'

Except for Jack's letters, I was entirely out of contact with the Marine Corps and our friends. My news of Korea was what I read in the papers, heard on the news and read in Jack's letters. That was enough. My job managed to put worry aside temporarily, but it always returned. The good news was that Jack was going to get an R&R in Japan in October. Seems that after 20 missions or so, an R&R was in order. Then came the word that Jack would be calling from Tokyo on such and such a day. Jack's parents lived in a rural community, and our phone number was 'four shorts on red.' That meant four short rings on the red line would get the Reeds. It also meant that other ears would be on the 'red' line. Well, our 'Central' was so excited that someone would be calling from Japan, she alerted the whole community. Jack's call came in, and everyone in Solon got plugged in on Jack's nickel. Only after an appeal did I get them to hang up so we could have our private moment. I heard the receivers click all down the line.

I was jolted when Jack wrote that he was going to be transferred from the squadron to the division as a forward air controller. It was the dead of winter, and I was well aware of what our Marines had gone through at the Chosin Reservoir. He reported to the division on the 1st of December 1951 and went to his unit, 2nd Battalion, 5th Marines, on Hill 884. My military lexicon was getting larger by the day. I breathed a little easier when he wrote that his unit would be going into reserve around Christmas. I sent more cookies. Thanks to a friendly battalion commander, Jack made another trip to Japan and ergo another community phone call. Seems that Jack was now the battalion club manager. I didn't understand all that was entailed, but it had something to do with setting up the 'O' club in reserve. I didn't complain. Four months later his FAC tour came to an end, and he was reassigned to Japan for the rest of his tour. Then the good news, orders arrived, and we were going back to Pensacola where Jack would be a flight instructor. He arrived home nine months after we said good-bye at El Toro and almost two years to the day after we left Camp Lejeune. He arrived home with an equal number of take-offs and landings and without a Purple Heart. I was one of the lucky ones.

Now, forty-five years later, this entire episode in my life seems like a blur and memory has dimmed the detail. I still have a sack full of letters with cartoons on the envelopes and sketches of his bunker somewhere out there and the 'free' instead of a stamp in the upper right corner. How could I have known that in all too short a time, I would be saying good-bye again, sending cookies to strange acronyms and hoping that my luck would hold.

The expression we have all heard, 'If the Corps had wanted Marines to have wives they would have been issued.' I know all the wives from that era would say, 'AMEN.'

BETTY MOORE

Christmas of 1950, Ben and I were living in Midway Island at Quantico, Virginia, when Ben got orders to Korea for August of 1951. First, though, he would go to artillery school at Fort Sill, Oklahoma.

We had just bought our first car, but I didn't know how to drive. I was about a month pregnant with our second child and wondered what I would do and where I would go. Since we barely had money for much, I decided to come back to Annapolis, where I would have lots of family support. After living with my brother and his family for a short time, I found an apartment two blocks from my mother and dad's home. The landlady was a widow with four apartments, and she rented me the one above her. She was willing to help me out whenever I needed her.

Ben managed to get leave after artillery school and was home for the birth of our daughter in early July. He left shortly thereafter for Korea.

My first project was to get my driver's permit, and once I got that, I was in the car all day, driving everyone anywhere they wanted to go.

The children and I took the train to Mississippi to visit Ben's mother and dad for Christmas. We stayed there for about a month before coming back to Annapolis.

The year went by quickly since I was in my hometown with my family and friends. I had all the military benefits offered by the naval station and the Naval Academy.

Ben wrote me almost every night, and I did the same. I can tell you, I lived for the sight of the mailman the entire time he was away. Sundays were always long because there wasn't any mail. One day, a military uniform got off a bus on the corner. Much to my surprise, it was Ben! I had no idea he was on his way home! After such a long separation, what a glorious day that was!

MARY GRATZER BUSH was teaching health and physical education at Mary Washington College in Virginia when she was introduced to a young marine lieutenant stationed at Basic School at Quantico, Virginia. Mary Washington was an all-girls school. Part of Mary's job was to serve as housemother for the young women. One girl in particular was staying out after hours with young marines. Mary reported this. The girl's idea was to get Mary and her watchful eye distracted and busy with a romance by introducing her to a young marine. The young marine turned out to be Clayton Bush. What was supposed to be a casual date turned into a lifelong romance.

When Basic School was over, Clayton was sent to Camp Pendleton, California. He and Mary had planned to be married in her hometown of Louisville, Kentucky, in August 1950. The outbreak of the Korean War changed their plans. They decided to set the date back and were married instead on July 17 of that year at the Santa Margarita Chapel in Pendleton. The chapel was a lovely wedding site, but since the couple didn't know many people, the wedding was small.

Lieutenant Bush wasn't sent to Korea until December. While they awaited his being shipped out, the newlyweds had five months together to adjust to married life and the impending separation. Mary had been in the Navy in World War II, so war and separation were not new to her

After Clayton left, Mary drove back across country. Another young wife and her children rode with her. Mary stayed with her parents until his return, which was all too soon. He was hit by shrapnel, which penetrated his wrist, severing a nerve and an artery. He was sent back to Memphis, Tennessee, close to Mary's home in Louisville. Fortunately, the doctors were able to repair the damage to his wrist, and he was able to finish his career in the Marine Corps.

At twenty-nine, Mary was older than some of her contemporaries, thus more experienced at coping with life. This was to stand her in good stead. She went through the ordeal of the separation from her husband and his subsequent wounding with bravery.

"My only reaction that was negative revolved around the fact that the letter notifying me of his having been wounded gave no facts and stated they would send more information concerning his whereabouts. The next information I received from the Marine Corps came weeks after we were together, and he had his surgery."

BOBBIE DOEZEMA

The Richard Doezemas were living in Jacksonville, North Carolina, when this country became involved in the Korean War. Dick was stationed at Camp Lejeune, and anticipating a tour of duty in the Second Marine Division, the Doezemas purchased a house along with another marine couple, Jack and Marion S. Nothing went as planned.

On short notice (six days), Dick was deployed, leaving Bobbie to arrange a move and rent the house along with the help of Marion. The wives picked up boxes from the quartermaster and packed themselves, storing the boxes temporarily in a spare bedroom in the house until the shippers could come.

Bobbie was expecting their second child. She was a month pregnant. Their daughter, Robin, was a year old. Bobbie and Dick had been married four years at this point.

Their car, a 1948 Hudson, was to serve as transportation back home for her and Robin, two other wives, and another one-year-old. The little group went as far as Quantico, Virginia, then went their separate ways. Back home for the Doezemas was Grand Rapids, Michigan. The boxes and the young family arrived safely—well, all except one box, which went to Iron Mountain, Michigan.

Bobbie and Robin lived for a time with her sister. She was, as she described all military families, poor as church mice. Later, she rented the house vacated by another sister whose husband had been called up by the marines. That was fine, except the heater went out in every strong wind. Thank heavens for a brother-in-law handyman! Finally, Bobbie and Robin moved in with her parents to help them manage their summer cottages. For prenatal care, Bobbie traveled seventy miles to an army hospital. Sharon, their second daughter, was born on March 12, 1951. Dick was still deployed.

After a separation of thirteen months, Dick returned. He had been twice wounded.

About this time, Bobbie says, "Some things were difficult, but this group of wives was capable and handled it well."

At just nineteen, **GLADYS "BABS" RUDZIS** was one of the youngest marine wives. She and Ed were living in Swansboro, North Carolina, just outside the marine base of Camp Lejeune. Ed had just transferred from infantry to artillery. There was no housing for newly arrived lieutenants and their families on the base, so they were living out in the civilian community in whatever was available. For the Rudzis, this was a little house on the inland waterway, within walking distance of Swansboro's one main street. The pay of a second lieutenant provided only a meager lifestyle, but the Rudzis managed.

Shortly, life was to be disrupted with the outbreak of the Korean War. Ed's battery was one of the first to be sent. He was gone thirteen months and returned with a souvenir—a metal cigarette case that he had carried under his clothing over his heart. The case bore the marks of a bullet that left two holes in all his garments but did not touch him.

Ed left, but Babs and Michael, their baby, had to wait for the movers. Everyone was packing and moving, so there was a delay during which Babs's mother stayed with her. Babs's parents drove down from Alexandria, Virginia. After the movers came, Babs and her mother drove back to Alexandria in the Rudzis' car. Babs and Michael lived in her parents' one-bedroom apartment. She kept busy with friends and volunteer activities as a grey lady at Bethesda Naval Hospital until she was reunited with Ed.

ANNA "PEGGY" SALVO and her one-year-old lived in Charleston, South Carolina, while they awaited Vic's return. He was deployed on a Mediterranean cruise. She was expecting their second child and was about to receive more than she expected.

Vic sent her the news that he was going straight from the ship to Korea, not returning home at all. At twenty-seven, and after three years of marriage, Peggy was prepared to cope. The couple had a car. Their finances were tolerable. She found an apartment in a housing complex. Their things were stored with a neighbor for the duration. Peggy let the neighbor know she needed a crib and baby things right away.

After ten months of separation, Vic returned home. He had been wounded but was okay.

A note from Peggy follows:

> Aug. 11, 1997
>
> Dear Adrienne,
>
> Sorry I've taken so long to answer but as you can see by my answers, I really had nothing to report. They really were cooperative about handling my move as they were very busy at that time.
>
> I have always felt the Marine Corps was cooperative in all my dealings with them.

Hope all is well with you & your family & again, my apology for taking so long to answer. Wish I had some exciting tales to tell. But at least I have no 'horror' stories.

Love,
Peggy Salvo

DORIE CARPER's remembrances of the early months of the Korean War 1950–51:

In July 1950 I was at Camp Pendleton, CA living in Homoja Housing, a large group of Quonset huts near the entrance to the front gate of the base. We lived in one-half of a Quonset, with two little girls, age two and six. Carole, the oldest, attended school in Oceanside. A half of a Quonset hut consisted of two very small bedrooms, one bathroom, shower only, the living room extended into a tiny kitchen. We had an icebox and an oil-burning space heater. All the curtains, or blinds, had to be attached to hooks on the walls because the walls were rounded. A blind came loose in our bedroom one night and in the moonlight I could see a small mouse swinging in the ring of the blind pull! Our bathroom door was open about two feet top and bottom so there wasn't much privacy. Our children would lie on the floor and talk to their Dad while he was using the facilities!! I bathed Dorinda, the two year old in the kitchen sink. She used a crib and our six year old slept on a regulation cot that was cut down to fit the small room. I was 24 years old. Dot Fredericks was one of my neighbors, also Gin Watterson was a friend living in Oceanside. One of my fondest or humorous memories was the 'Wash House' where we carried our laundry. I think there were six or eight washing machines, full every morning, but available in late afternoon. I can't remember dryers, but we put up clotheslines, and I let nature dry mine! The 'Wash House' was our news and gossip center while we waited for our laundry to be finished. Seldom did you enter it that soap suds weren't running out the door!! My mother visited us (somehow we fit another cot in the children's bedroom), and she always remembered her visits to the 'Wash House' with me, she found it fascinating with all the little kids running around, and the mounds of soap suds!!

'Carp' and I had been married nearly seven years, he was 25 years old and a First Lieutenant. On the 4th of July 1950 the Marines of the 1st Marine Division were gathered on the parade ground for a parade and review. Then, to everyone's surprise, it was announced that a Brigade would be formed and leave for Korea as soon as it was organized. This was accomplished by the 13th of July. Needless to say, our life was in turmoil. Also in that week my sister and brother-in-law were visiting us from Pennsylvania, they had come to pick up my mother who had been with us for a month. The Marines of the Brigade were shipping out from San Diego, and I and a friend, June, drove down to spend the evening with our husbands and say a tearful 'good-bye' but not before having 'an evening on the town' as they say. My family, thankfully were there, to care for our daughters because it was early AM when Carp and Dave boarded the U.S.S. *Clymer* and June and I returned to Camp Pendleton. My family drove back to PA without me because I made the decision to stay on the West Coast. The Marine Corps announced shortly after that wives had thirty days to vacate Homoja Housing. Amazingly, we didn't whine, we didn't cry, we didn't write letters, we just picked ourselves up, acted like adult women and searched for housing elsewhere, mainly Oceanside. I'm sure in today's world we would have had lawyers knocking at our doors encouraging us to file a class action lawsuit against the Marine Corps for shabby treatment, even the ACLU may have taken up our plight!! Such litigation never occurred to me. I wasn't angry with anyone, this was Marine Corps life. My husband was facing a far more perilous situation, and heartbreak to see him go far outweighed any anger.

Dot Fredericks, who had a 3 year old daughter, and I joined together and searched for a house to share in Oceanside. Rents seemed high for a single income. We answered several ads in the Oceanside paper, but it became clear, that in the sections of the city where we preferred to live, landlords weren't amenable to renting to two single women with three children. Dot found an attractive condo right on the ocean, and I moved into a single house a block away with an affordable rent. I did have to go to the Navy Relief Society for a loan for furniture. The Quonset huts were government furnished. In those days we lived from payday to payday, with little, if any, savings. And with the sudden departure of my husband and pay checks fouled up I needed financial help. There were just six houses on my street, and the neighbors were very helpful. A Navy man hung curtain rods for me. Sheets that I hung at night and removed during the day were adequate until I found drapes at a thrift store. My circle of friends, Marine wives that I previously mentioned, made the daily responsibilities easier. I also had a car and could take advantage of the hospital, PX, and commissary at Camp Pendleton. My six year old daughter contracted the mumps, one side only, but when the bug caught me I swelled on both sides and was quite ill and confined to the house. With my friends coming to the window to check on me and drop off food, I muddled through. Thankfully, the bug skipped my two year old. Especially during the Chosin Reservoir battle, the 5 O'clock radio news (no TV then) with Chet Huntley and David Brinkley was my link to Korea. Letters were very scarce and when they reported Marine activities, I (and the other wives) had some clue where the men were. One of the greatest fears was finding a Western Union person at your door with a telegram. That was the way your husband's death or wounding was reported. I never received one, thank God. But a friend of mine from PA was visiting in Los Angeles, and since coming to California back then was an event in my small town in PA, she sent me a telegram to announce that she had made it to CA!! That was the closest I came to fainting. I chastised her in a letter, explaining what a faux pas she had made. My most anxious days were those waiting to hear if the 1st Marine Division, surrounded by the Chinese at the Chosin Reservoir could fight their way out. They did and then came the news that 'Carp' was coming home. I dressed my daughters and myself in our finest and met his ship in San Diego in May 1951. What a glorious reunion!! Then we packed up and headed for Parris Island, SC.

Without that small circle of Marine wives to share those long, lonely and anxious days and share a laugh or tear with, life would have been very bleak. Some are still very good friends and we keep in touch with them and their husbands.

MEMORIES OF THE KOREAN WAR

LAURA L. REEVES

In March 1950, we were stationed at Marine Corps Recruit Depot (MCRD) San Diego, California. We were only there for a short time. Orders came. The new duty station was Camp Lejeune, North Carolina. With our twenty-two-month-old son and the second child due in May, we drove to Florida, where another son was born. Adolph (my husband) rented the upstairs of a nice partly furnished old home in Richlands, North Carolina, perhaps thirteen miles from Camp Lejeune. Base housing was not easy to obtain. The babies and I joined Adolph as soon as I could travel. At this time, I was twenty-three years of age. Adolph was twenty-seven.

In July (not sure of the date), Adolph came home with news that he was deployed. This was Wednesday. We called his parents and asked them to come up and help with the move back to Florida and, of course, see Adolph before he left. Wednesday to Sunday was a busy, hectic few days with little time for each other and family. I washed, heavy-starched, and ironed several sets of fatigues. He was at camp long hours each day.

On Sunday morning, he was on a troop train headed for Camp Pendleton, California. Our fourth wedding anniversary would be October 25, 1950.

I rented a small apartment in Orlando, Florida. We were only there a short time and moved to another small apartment in Winter Garden, Florida, close to his parents and other family. My family was also not far away.

Our financial circumstances were not great, but I managed. Dolph was a staff sergeant in the Marine Corps. Pay was low—very low—in those days. We owned a car. I could drive, so that helped, making it easy to visit my mother, sisters, and their families. My brother was in the Air Force, stationed in Macon, Georgia. He would come down on weekends and help with the children and—oh yes—my car.

The troop train took our marine to Camp Pendleton, California. where he joined the First Marine Division. I'm not sure the exact date in July they left San Diego, California, by ship for Japan before going to Korea.

We wrote each day. Dolph was good to let me know where he was and how he was. After awhile, words such as *Seoul*, *Wonson*, *Puson*, *Mason*, *Sudong*, *Youdam-ni*, *Chosin Reservoir*, *Hamhung*, and more (perhaps not in that order) became familiar. Places I had never heard of.

The war goes on. A short time after Thanksgiving, I received no mail—no word whatsoever—as to how he was or where he was! Without his letters, each day became more difficult—not knowing if he was dead or alive. News as we know it today just did not exist in 1950. Radio, paper, *Life*, and *Look* magazine did a good job. Each week, I would be at the corner drugstore for my copy of *Life* and *Look* magazines, in hopes I'd see a picture that Adolph would be in or something that would help. Pictures, yes, but none of Dolph! Without word from him, each day became a blur. One day ran into the next. At times, the dishes were left. All I could do was see the babies were cared for. I gave up the apartment and moved in with Mom and Dad (Adolph's parents). They were of much help and comfort. We were all so worried, not knowing if he was dead, alive, wounded, or captured. What we did hear and read was about the cold, frozen land. What little news we received was not good. Still no mail! I was at a real low.

It was time to decorate and plan for Christmas. We felt we could not even think of the holidays. Then, on Christmas Eve, a letter arrived saying he was alive and not wounded. I believe at this time, the troops had gone aboard ship. They had survived what we now know all so well as the Chosin Reservoir. We did cheer up, put out a few Christmas decorations, and celebrated our wonderful news and made Christmas for the two young children.

I will forever be most grateful for the marine officers in charge of troops that brought so many out of the Chosin. I still feel sad for those that never returned.

In January 1951, I sent Adolph a small leather-bound New Testament for his twenty-eighth birthday. I opened it and saw Psalm 27, first verse: "The Lord is my light and my salvation; whom shall I fear? The Lord is the strength of my life, of whom shall I be afraid?" I marked those words and wrote inside the cover, "To Adolph—Jan. 15, 1951—My Love Always, Your Wife, Laura." I cannot say if he read the psalm, but I can say they stayed with me during those lonely days. It's now 2001. The little black worn leather New Testament is still with me. I often read or repeat those words I marked in 1951.

The most difficult time was the three weeks or so that I did not hear from Dolph, wondering if he was dead or alive. After the men got out of the Chosin, someone took these pictures of Dolph and gave them to him. On the back of the pictures, the person had written the pictures were taken at Sudong or Hamhung after the Chosin operation. Adolph sent the pictures to me, telling me he was eating frozen rations. I would cry when looking at them. He looked so worn, dirty, and old for a twenty-eight-year-old.

In early 1951, I took a job in Orlando. Mom and Dad cared for the growing boys. I needed something to help take my thoughts off the war—plus, we needed the money, little as it was. We were making plans for me to meet Dolph in California when he returned to the States. No information on ship movements was out, so in August 1951, I went to Vista, California, by Greyhound bus. I was with a friend, also a marine wife.

Adolph called, telling me he was in Treasure Island, California. I flew (my first time) to San Francisco. He met me at the airport. We had a wonderful few days in San Francisco even though he was on duty. We traveled back to Florida—yes, by Greyhound bus—to prepare for the drive back to Camp Pendleton, California, with our two little ones.

Wives in those days were separated in so many cases. We did not have each other like couples today. If a wife received any special treatment, I was not aware of it. We were pretty much forgotten unless the recipient of bad news. So like those I know, we accepted what we had to do and did it. In some cases, we went home to family or where we could be settled when our marine returned. I keep in touch with some of these wives today and know of not one that complained. Like our marines, we were just doing what we had to do. We could at least stay warm and not be in the danger they were in.

In 1950, I was a young wife and knew so little about the Marine Corps. Did I complain? I don't think at any time of Dolph's twenty-six years of active duty. He was a marine by choice through World War II, Korea, and Vietnam. He retired from the corps on 31 July 1968. Would I have changed my life as a marine wife if I could? I would not. Yes, war is so very awful for all—being separated for long periods, being alone with children to care for, and the loneliness. That was my job while he did his job being a marine, realizing he was also lonely.

Staff Sergeant Reeves.

BARBARA REID SORENSEN

"I think it was July 4, 1950 when Wally learned he was going to Korea. Wally was stationed at Camp Pendleton. I was twenty-six years old. We had been married five years. Like most of our friends we lived from month to month and had no savings."

Barbara and Wally met in Tacoma, Washington. Barbara was working and going to college. Wally was a marine on leave in 1942. He returned to the Pacific theater. They corresponded until he returned in November of 1944 and dated until March of 1945, when they married. After finishing Fifth Basic School, Quantico, Virginia, Wally was sent to Pendleton. Barbara, Wally, and Wallace Jordan Reid II, then two, moved into quarters. Barbara was pregnant with their second child. Wally was stationed aboard a submarine, outward-bound for Alaska and Hawaii. He was home for the birth of Randall Earl Reid. Unfortunately, during the weekend Barbara and the new baby came home from the hospital, food poisoning sickened the new mom and put Wally in the hospital. All soon recovered.

After Wally was deployed to Korea, his mother came down from Washington State to drive back with Barbara and the two little boys, who were sixteen months apart. Barbara lived with her mother but, ultimately, bought a house. Both mother and mother-in-law were near. They worked. When the boys were three and two, Barbara went back to work. She eventually finished college.

Wallace Jordan Reid was killed in action on August 8, 1950.

Barbara remarried after the boys were out of high school. When I asked about the hardships she had endured, she replied, "This is what made us who we are."

DOROTHY "DOT" FREDERICKS

(MRS. HAROLD D.)

Separation was not a new experience for Dottie and Bud Fredericks. As a newlywed, Dot had seen Bud off for a tour of duty in China. Then upon his return, Bud was injured in a truck accident. At least those previous separations had prepared Dot to make the right decision where to locate with Wendy, their one-year-old daughter, in Bud's absence.

Dot's mother was visiting from Massachusetts. To her, it seemed best for Dot and Wendy to return to Massachusetts with her. Despite the mother's well-intentioned pleas, Dottie felt she would be happier close to other marine wives who were staying in Oceanside until their husbands returned. As Dottie put it, "We were a sisterhood. If one of us got down, there were the others to cheer her up." After all, Dottie had gone home when Bud was sent to China. She learned from that experience how lonely it could be, isolated in a civilian community as the only military wife.

The couple and Wendy were living in Homoja at Camp Pendleton when his orders came. Orders for Bud meant relocation for his wife since the family had to move out of government housing shortly after the deployment of the husband. Dottie found an ideal duplex right on the beach. It belonged to a Hollywood set designer. Transportation was no problem since they had purchased a new car, but the car payment was a challenge on an allotment. Sometimes there was more month than money.

Bud was wounded in Korea in August when the jeep he was riding in hit a landmine. Dot was notified but not told of the category of the wound. She was trying to call Japan to get information when the grapevine provided her with the nature of the wound. He did not have to be evacuated. She had had a nightmare the night before she got the message. In her dream, Bud was calling her. Bud came home in March when so many other marines returned. The troop ship docked at San Francisco. Dottie and Gin Watterson were there. A photographer recorded the hugs and kisses.

What follows are excerpts from letters Dot wrote her mother at this time. She is generously sharing them with us. As we read them, I'm sure we will recognize and remember what we went through during that winter long ago.

LETTERS TO DOTTIE FREDERICK'S MOTHER

Friday, November 3, 1950

Dear Mom and Rudy,

Well, I needn't tell you that the war situation is really grim. You know that if you have been listening to the radio or reading the papers these past few days.

My last letters received from Bud were written the 16, 17, and 18th of October. He was preparing to make the landing at Wonsan and was still aboard ship at the time. His letters were very optimistic, and he thought he'd be coming home very soon. [Ed. note: Even General MacArthur was saying some of the boys would be back by Thanksgiving.] I wonder how his morale is today. I know it must be at an all time low. I don't expect him home for Xmas now—nor do I expect him for months after—Lord only knows when the war will end. It certainly looks today like the beginning of a 3rd World War. [Ed. note: It was at this time that the war had moved beyond the 38th parallel and the Chinese had entered the fray. Cutoff at the Chosin Reservoir lay ahead.]

I hope I'm being overly pessimistic and that it does not come to pass—but it seems inevitable. Don't say 'I told you so' because this Chinese intervention came as a shock to all the top brass at this late date. However, that is what has turned the tide.

Everyone here has had the wind knocked out of our sails. We're all feeling just sick to death, but there's not a thing we can do. I wonder if there is still any hope left in us. There was yesterday—but today it's even worse. Guess the right thing to do is to force ourselves not to give up hope. It looks futile now, but it's always darkest before dawn, or worse before good, or something to that effect.

I had a fairly nice birthday. Nothing gala, that is in the way of celebration, but I did get some nice gifts. Mrs. Fredericks sent me a nylon slip and two pairs of nylon panties. Bud's aunt sent me 3 pairs of nylon hose. His cousin, Ronnie, sent me a beautiful blue nightgown with lace trim. Pat C. (girlfriend in Conn.) sent a huge bouquet of flowers. And Dad called from Rockville, and we talked for about 20 minutes or more on Sunday night.

Haven't done much for excitement. Have company just about everyday, and when they aren't here I visit them. Joyce moved into one of the houses near Gin and Kay—those cute gray and white ones—and she has her place looking quite lovely. She finally got all her gear from Japan, and she has some beautiful things. She should be much happier there than in that other drab, bare place.

Wendy is fine and getting cuter by the day. She runs like lightning now, and I really have to travel to keep up with her. Tuesday being Halloween night I dressed her up like a bunny, and Dorie and Joyce and I took our kids 'trick or treating.' She looked just adorable, and everyone raved about her. I put her pink pajamas on and sewed big pink terry cloth ears to a pink helmet type bonnet she has. Lined them with cardboard so that they stood up straight. Pinned a big wad of cotton to her fanny for a tail, and she'd have won any prize going. Took some pictures for Bud and everyone; so, I'm hoping they turn out good. By 8:30 when we got home she was so tired and full of candy. The cardboard had gone limp, and the ears flopped down over her eyes like cheaters. But even then she looked more comical than ever.

Hope you haven't been worrying about the flood waters reaching Oceanside. Wonder if the East Coast papers have played up the California floods. The war news is only secondary here now. I guess the floods are pretty bad, lots of damages done to crops and homes. But there's little chance of it doing any damage here. We have had very little rain. It has been drizzly for the past four days, but the sun comes out for an hour or so during the day.

Guess that is about all for now. Think I'll take a run down to Gin's and see if she got any mail. Joyce's mother and father were here from Texas for a week but have gone back now. Gin's mother and father were out too from Detroit.

Write soon. Regards to all. And I hope you all have a very nice Thanksgiving.

Love,
Dot and Wendy

• •

Monday, December 4, 1950

Dear Mom,

Sorry I haven't written—I know you have been worried about the news and everything. But I just couldn't get myself to write letters. Of course, I too am very worried and scared stiff. It's a horrible thing that is happening—it doesn't seem possible that it can be true.

It's going to be a long, worried wait till I get mail from Bud again to know that he is all right. He is in one of the Marine Regiments trapped around the Changjhin (Chosin) Reservoir. I hear on the radio they got out of that trap today with heavy casualties but still have to break thru more traps to reach the sea, where I assume they will be evacuated by ship.

My last letter was written on Nov. 21, and of course none of this had happened at that time.

Don't worry about me. I'll be okay. I realize more each day that I mustn't break down or get sick—for Wendy's sake. So I force myself to eat, and I try not to stay in the house alone and brood. All we girls feel the same way; so, we try to stay together to get each others' minds off our husbands. No one is better off than the next one. But I think it helps to be miserable together. I'd really go insane with worry and fright if I were home and so alone in the thing. I wonder how June and Connie are taking it.

However, it looks more and more everyday as if we will be involved, or rather, 'at' war with China. Possibly by the time this letter reaches you. If it is all out war, then I think I have made up my mind to return home.

Guess once more I must say you were right all along. Yet I don't regret having stayed here this long—not one minute of it. And if by some miracle this thing can be ironed out peaceably, then I shall remain here to go on waiting for Bud. But nevertheless I have been giving it considerable thought.

I'll ask no help from anyone back home this time. If I do come East I will do it completely my own. There will perhaps be other girls going East in such an event, and we will work out something. I'm not going to worry about that—in addition to my worry about Bud. He is utmost in my mind today. Of course, I realize there is nothing I can do for him here and that Wendy should be my chief concern because I certainly can help her. She is fine and healthy, tho I think she must sense the tension as she is quite whiney and begs to be picked up a lot. I'm just glad that she isn't old enough to understand.

Don't know how we'll get thru this Xmas, but we have all agreed that we will make the best of it. I'll have a tree, and trim it and try to make it nice for Wendy. I have all her gifts bought so will be spared the trying ordeal of having to do it now at this time. I lack even the slightest trace of Xmas spirit this year, and I get no pleasure whatsoever out of shopping. Maybe if the news will get brighter I will be able to go about it a little more cheerfully.

Love,
Dot and Wendy

• •

Monday, Dec. 11, 1950

Dear Mom,

Just received your letter; so, will answer immediately while Wendy is taking her nap. I know you have been worried, and I have wanted to write but hardly wrote a line to anyone—even Bud—while the news was so bad. But the news is better now, and they are out of that horrible trap. One phase of it is over. However, now I'm back in the state where my heart pounds for minutes each time the doorbell rings. I got over that shortly after you left, but I'm scared all over again. The casualties were the Marine Corps highest, and the telegrams will start flowing in soon.

DEAR GOD! I hope He is good to me and will not send me one. One of our friends got the fatal news already. You never met her.

Another girl—Betty—you did meet her—her husband is coming home this week. He was wounded a few months ago and sent to Japan. At least he'll be coming home. He's okay now. Shrapnel in his fanny.

All the other girls are okay—all nervous and waiting anxiously for a letter from our husbands saying they are okay. If Buddy got thru that deal all right, I shall never consider us unlucky again.

I'm waiting for Cookie to arrive today. Got a special delivery letter this morning saying she would come today. I'm anxious to see her.

Art and Gen are here and are living in the hut next door to mine at Homoja. It doesn't look as tho Art will be going overseas with this bunch this month and maybe not for quite some time. He may be sent to a school in Oklahoma for 6 to 9 months.

Most all of the husbands of the wives you met were in around the Changjin Reservoir trap. With the exception of Kay's husband who is a flyer. Bev, next door, has been receiving mail everyday from hers; so, he is okay. He's at Hamhung. Dorie's husband was out of it till her last letter of Dec 2nd when he wrote that he was being sent up to the front—probably as part of the rescue relief column. Most everyone else was in the thick of it with Bud.

Guess I hadn't told you he is no longer with Headquarters. He was right in the front with them all. Even if he were at Hdqtrs., he wouldn't be any safer than anyone else under those conditions. He is working in a company now and has been for about two months. It was upsetting news when he told me because I always felt he was a little safer being back with the battalion command post. However, the day after he was transferred and sent forward the battalion C.P. was ambushed by the enemy. He didn't say if they suffered any losses, but it was perhaps fortunate that he had been transferred that day. I have high hopes that once evacuated from Korea the Marines will not have to go back in again. It would be brutal to send those men in again after what they have just been thru. This war is so damn futile! I think we should get out of Korea all together and let it sink or swim. It's about time we started taking care of our own skins! That 'G.D.' Truman is such an asinine fool, he and all his dimwits in Washington make my blood boil. He's crazy if he doesn't allow those troops to get out of Korea—he's already got the blood of thousands of G.I.'s on his hands. I owe June a letter but can't write till I learn Bud is okay. Connie owes me one—wonder how she is. Dave must have been stuck in the trap too because he is in Bud's outfit. Dick is with the 1st Marine Regiment, and they were in Koto.

I will send my Xmas box off to you this week. The gifts are not as nice as I would like to send, but I hope you will understand. I'm managing my finances okay, but I will admit it is not as easy as I thought it would be.

Christmas is only two weeks away—I'm not looking forward to it, but I'm not dreading it either. I'll have a tree, and it will be fun for Wendy when she sees her tricycle and gifts in the morning. We girls are having a few parties during the holidays; so, maybe it won't be too lonesome without the fellows if we can get together and occupy our minds on something else. Dorie is having the gang over next Friday. Gin is having open house on Xmas Day, and Joyce is having a party sometime between Xmas and New Years.

Wendy is fine—eating like a horse and getting taller and fatter. She's still not 'fat,' just nice. Still whines a lot, however, to the point of driving me crazy. But she's still a doll, and as angry as she makes me sometimes I'd be lost without her. Did I tell you I bought her a new red coat and hat for Xmas. Gee, she looks so cute in it— bright red with imitation grey Persian lamb on the collar. It was a bargain, and I couldn't resist it. Must close.

Love to all,
Dot and Wendy

P.S. You've been asking about the weather; so, here's the report (which reminds me—the Welcome Wagon Lady, Mrs Murphy, always asks about you whenever I see her. Says she bets you wish you were still in California to enjoy this nice weather.) And it has been nice, too. Temperatures range somewhere in the 80s. Sun is out most everyday, but some days we do have considerable fog. People are still in swimming down on the beach on warm days. The evenings are quite chilly and damp—heavy dew on everything by 5:00 p.m. I haven't been swimming for quite some time.

The tide comes up quite high now—almost to where the green ends down on the beach. And you never saw it go out as far as it does now. Way, way out! The waves are seldom any higher than usual and never high enough to scare me. Up at Redondo Beach (near L. A.), they have been having 18 feet waves that lash the shore on bad days, never anything like that here. It's a known fact that the waves are rather dangerous at Redondo Beach every year at this time.

Mrs. Willis is still watching every move from her window. Haven't been over to see her for some time as I'm too busy visiting the girls. When I feel low I rush down to Gin's, and she talks me out of it. She never shows her worry and always makes me feel better. Or we get together at Dorie's or Kay's and gripe about the way the war is being fought. Seems as tho Cookie should have arrived by now. Not yet, however.

Don't worry about Wendy and me, Mom. We're okay, and when I get that letter from Bud assuring me he's okay, I'll do flip-flops for joy! Mrs. Fredericks felt pretty bad last week, but in her letter today she said she had pulled herself together. She asked for you and says she means to write to you everyday but like me, can't bring herself to write to anyone these days. She hopes you will understand, and she will write as soon as she can.

Regards to Gram and Gramps and all.

Love,
Dot and Wendy

P. S. Gloria finally got around to writing a brief one or two page letter awhile ago. Not a line from brother Bob.

• •

Saturday, December 23, 1950

Dear Mom and Rudy,

BUDDY IS SAFE! I got a letter, or rather three letters from him on Thursday. They were written on board ship as they were being evacuated from Hungnam. He is now at Pusan—right back where they started when he first landed in Korea on August 2nd. He said the whole retreat from the Reservoir was a horrible nightmare. He wrote me all about it as soon as he got to the port—said he'd feel better after he got it all off his chest. God was certainly by his side. Out of his battalion of 900 men only 300 came thru. Not all of the casualties were dead—many had frostbite, sores, etc. It was on one of the first days of the retreat that he took over the dreaded job of rifle platoon leader. I have always feared that as it is about the most dangerous. He had 44 men under him, and after about four days he had only 13 left. I hope and pray he gets another job when they reorganize—tho I guess that last episode proves that it's not the kind of job you have, but rather whether or not it is meant that you pull thru.

One of our friend's husband was killed. Wanda (You met her.)—she was pregnant when you saw her last. Her husband is the one whose first wife died last year about the time Bud had his accident. Now he leaves Wanda and a son Wendy's age and a baby girl he has never seen. It's too awful to be true. All we girls know about it, but so far Wanda doesn't. She went to live with her mother about 200 miles from here and apparently hasn't been notified yet. We learned of it thru letters from some of the fellows with him.

Dick C. was wounded slightly on or about Dec. 3 according to Connie's last letter. But it wasn't serious enough to take him out of battle. I hope he came thru the rest of the way okay. I'll bet Connie was sick with worry. Dave is okay. He was in Bud's battalion, and Bud says he is all right. All the other wives have heard from their husbands; so, there has been much rejoicing here now that the tension is over, and we know they are okay. I'm ever so grateful! I feel like a new person.

You asked about Cookie. She is living in San Diego with Tom—when he isn't out to sea. His orders to leave Jan. 3 were cancelled, but they don't know how long he'll be here. They are coming up Xmas Day. I'm having them and the Larievys here for a baked ham dinner.

It looks as tho Wendy will have a Merry Xmas at any rate. She has oodles of presents already, and yours and Dad's haven't even arrived yet. I got some, too, but I still won't be able to enjoy Christmas knowing Bud is over there instead of with us. I have a Xmas tree and the presents are bulging off the edges of the table and even underneath.

Grandma sent $5; so, I bought Wendy some pajamas and loafer socks to slip over her p.j.'s in the morning. She loves the slippers. I tried them on her, and she wouldn't take her eyes off them.

Mr. and Mrs. Kish, the landlords, sent Bev and me each a beautiful poinsettia plant for Xmas. Wasn't that nice of them?

No, I don't think I would consider going back with Cookie unless a war broke out. I'd dread the trip by car at this time of the year. If Bud isn't home by June, then I may attempt the drive, but that's too far ahead to plan.

Don't get any mad ideas about pulling strings to get Bud out of Korea. No strings Mr. Fredericks or Mrs. Fredericks or all their friends in Washington could pull would get him out. His case is no different than a lot of others. Not only that, but I know Bud wouldn't want any strings pulled to get him out. No Marine would.

[Ed. note: At this point, part of the letter is missing.]

Wonder if Bob is home now. Lucky guy! Wish I were home—especially over the holidays. Couldn't help but feel terribly homesick tonight as I looked out on a very dense fog and wished I was looking on a snow-covered countryside. It's just not Christmassy in California.

I'd sure love to show Wendy off. Boy is she getting to be a little imp these days. She teases me no end. Keeps getting out of bed once she's in for the night or keeps playing with her food—all the time looking at me with the most devilish eyes waiting for me to make the next move. She knows I can't do anything but smile when she gives me that look out of the corner of her eyes. I hope she doesn't forget that cute trick before her Daddy comes home. I do so want him to see her go into her act. Course it doesn't always win me over—she does get a spanking occasionally.

Hope you and Rudy have a very Merry Christmas, and I sincerely hope and pray that next year will be a happier and better one for us all. Regards and Merry Christmas to everyone.

[The rest of the letter is missing.]

MARY WHITE LUCY

(MRS. ROBERT)

Mary White was perhaps the only wife of a member of the First Marine Brigade who was allowed to remain in Sterling Housing, a government facility, after the men deployed. The reason for this was medical. Mary White was pregnant with their first child, and her doctor forbade travel for three months. She moved in with another wife for several months when Bob left with his unit for Korea.

Prior to this, the Lucys had been living "the good life" in an apartment on the beach in Oceanside. They had been married three years. Mary White was twenty when they got married. They had no children as yet, and when Bob left, they did not know whether or not Mary White was pregnant.

Eventually, Mary White was able to make the trip home. Her mother-in-law came out to California, and they drove home in the Lucys' car. Mary White stayed for the duration with her parents in Columbus, Tennessee. When Bob came home, he was greeted by Mary White and a baby daughter.

Mary White felt welcomed by her parents, making the inevitable anxiety and loneliness, which all the wives experienced, easier to bear. "I realize how fortunate I was compared to other wives who had financial problems, the responsibility of children, no support system, no place to move."

BETTY J. LEES, her husband, Gordon, and their two children, six and one and a half, were in Tucson, Arizona, when the United States became involved in the Korean War. The couple had been married since 1943.

Gordon was an army combat engineer attached to a civilian component. When he got orders to Korea, they drove to Travis Air Force Base, where Gordon left. He got to Korea in time for the landing at Inchon. Betty's mother met her in California and accompanied Betty and the children home.

> Betty writes,
>
> My two children and I stayed with my folks in Montana when Gordon went to Korea. Thank God for my parents! When reports started coming from the war that were not good, I became a basket case. My parents wouldn't let me read the paper or listen to the radio. Also they helped me make Christmas for the children. Finally in January I got a letter from Gordon with these words, 'Got out OK.' on the outside of the envelope. We all celebrated! My heart goes out to the widows and mothers whose loved ones didn't get out 'OK.'
>
> Gordon was in the Army Engineers, X Corps. The picture was taken when he was evacuated at

Hungnam. The ship is a freighter. I asked him why he couldn't remember the name of the ship, and he said he was more interested in getting out than the ship's name!

Gordon Lees

Hungnam

Port

Leaving harbor

Courtesy of Gordon Lees

BETTY BEY

August 27, 2002

It all seems so long ago since I became a Marine Corps wife. Why should it not? It has been fifty-seven-plus years. Bob graduated from OCS on June 20, 1945. We married in Alexandria, Virginia, the following day. (My father was at the Pentagon in those days, and I'd been living with my parents.) After our honeymoon, Bob left for Camp Lejeune, and I continued living with my parents. Once he found a place for us to live, I followed him to Camp Lejeune. I loved my new life there. It was so different from anything I'd known—the officers club, the beautiful beach, many new friends, etc. It was a dream come true. I was so very much in love.

After a few months there, Bob was sent to Camp Pendleton, and I, of course, followed shortly after. We lived in several places and finally got an adorable little apartment right on the beach. I loved it. Bob was released to inactive duty in the reserve. That was December 1945. I was pregnant at that time. We journeyed back to the East Coast via train.

I stayed (again) with my parents until Barbara was born in June 1946. Bob began college in Cleveland,

Ohio, in the spring quarter, and we were on a waiting list for government housing. My parents returned to Ohio in the late summer of 1946—Barbara and I with them. She and I soon went to Cleveland. We lived in a one-bedroom third-floor apartment in public housing in the black district until Bob's graduation in 1948. We paid $24 a month on rent. (Bob's folks helped us out with $50 per month.) Bob was in the organized reserve throughout '47 and '48.

After graduation, Bob was hired as management trainee by Western Auto Supply Company, first in Cleveland and then in Barberton, Ohio, an Akron suburb. He became assistant manager of the larger Akron store in '49 and then manager of the store in Warren, Ohio, in the early summer of '50.

Our second daughter, Deborah, was born in June 1949. Bob was in the organized reserve in Akron through August '50 and commuted from Warren once or twice a week. We were in the process of buying a house in Warren. The girls and I continued living near Akron.

Then came June 25, 1950. The Akron reserve organization was activated in late July or early August and prepared to go to Camp Pendleton. And now my story begins. I was twenty-five years old and knew my husband would be leaving for Korea. We had been married five years. I really was in a quandary as to what to do or where I should go. However, after much urging from both Bob's parents and my own, we decided the girls and I would be best off to stay right there in Zanesville, Ohio, where both families lived.

My parents found us a small but very nice apartment very near the school where my father taught high school chemistry. He was a great help to me as he'd walk over for lunch, and we'd have some adult conversation—something my life lacked with two little girls, ages one and a half and four. Bob bid us good-bye and left with the reserve unit from Akron in late August.

In early September, I flew out to Pendleton for a few weeks with Bob, staying in Oceanside, where we had lived previously. My parents were kind enough to keep the girls for me.

I recall vividly how no one in the small town other than both sets of parents even seemed to know there was a Korea etc. I did have one friend, a divorcee, who lived in the apartment above me with whom I was friendly. But with no other friends, I was very lonely and worried so about Bob. His parents helped by sending Barbara to a private kindergarten, which she enjoyed, and that made life a bit easier for me. Christmas was coming and reports from Korea were dire, and I worried even more than before. Most folks around us were wondering 'Just what Santa will bring?' and 'Will my wishes be granted?' The girls and I would often go to our parents, but otherwise, the three of us were pretty much alone, just waiting for word from Bob.

Since I didn't drive, we had sold our car, so we had no transportation. The school bus would come for Barbara, which was a great help, and of course, our parents helped when asked. I would put Debbie in the old-fashioned metal Taylor-Tot, and with Barbara's 'help,' we'd often go uptown. That was only six to eight blocks from home. We did lots and lots of shop-looking. I can't recall having money problems—Bob would send what he could from Korea, and I really had little I needed except for food and diapers. I really missed Marine Corps wives and knew then I'd do differently should there be another deployment. I also found I was pregnant for a third time. This was quite a surprise, but a welcome one, as our girls were my delight. My folks heard of a house for rent quite near them. They helped us move. Being near them was such a help to me. Bob often says, at that time, he was the only man in Korea who didn't know where he lived for I'd written we had moved but failed to say exactly where or when.

I'd always dreaded going to our front door and finding a telegram. Bob was wounded on 6 December '50 on the way out of the reservoir. I didn't get word of it until later as Bob continued out of the reservoir instead of going to an aid station, where a casualty report would have been made. Bob wrote me of this. Since he himself had written, I felt much assured of his condition. It was good being near my parents, for they helped so much with the girls, and the three of us enjoyed being around them. My grandmother was living at that time, and she was an angel to us.

I did receive the dreaded telegram on January 30, when Bob was wounded again and evacuated to Japan. It was very upsetting for several days until I had a follow-up report, but when I did, I heard he was doing well and would be coming home soon. He arrived on 20 March '51, and we were all so happy to see him. We were so thankful we were a family once again. He was ordered to recruiting duty in Cleveland and got a regular commission. Our third daughter, Elayne, was born in a Zanesville hospital, and about a month later, Bob came and took us to our home there. Of course, he had been there for Elayne's birth.

Yes, it was a lonely time for me, but I tried not to complain as I knew Bob was having a rough time. Marine Corps life was one of the happiest times I can remember. I haven't regretted it for a minute, and we have met so many great people, many with whom we keep in touch

This was a different lifestyle from most during that time, but I never let it happen again. Later, I always stayed around good friends for support and camaraderie, but I also feel I did the right thing at that time.

Mrs. Robert "Betty" Bey

TALENTS

God has gifted each marine wife
With a talent that is unique.
It is theirs to share with others,
Or theirs to decide to keep.
So nourish it and make it grow,
And in every way give praise.
In the darkness of the night,
In the brightness of the days.
This talent that was given to you,
Came from our God above.
It is a true reflection,
Of our Heavenly Father's love.

So use your talent as best you can.
Share it with others each day.
Offer it up to God our Father.
That is how you pray.
Remember that you are special.
You are blessed on this earthly scene.
You have been given an important role.
You are the wife of a United States Marine.
So use your talent as best you can.
Share it with others each day.
Offer it up to God our Father.
That is how you pray.

—Estelle Deptula

www.ingramcontent.com/pod-product-compliance
Ingram Content Group UK Ltd.
Pitfield, Milton Keynes, MK11 3LW, UK
UKHW041936190726
13854UKWH00004B/1611

9 781483 607085